WARREN
BUFFETT

Financier

Bernard Ryan, Jr.

Ferguson
An imprint of ☑️ Facts On File

Warren Buffett: Financier

Ferguson
An imprint of Facts On File, Inc.
132 West 31st Street
New York NY 10001

Library of Congress Cataloging-in-Publication Data

Ryan, Bernard, 1923–
  Warren Buffett : financier / Bernard Ryan
      p. cm.
  Includes index
  ISBN 0-8160-5894-6 (hc. : alk. paper)
  1. Buffett, Warren—Juvenile literature. 2. Capitalists and financiers—United States—Biography—Juvenile literature. 3. Stockbrokers—United States—Biography—Juvenile literature. I. Title.
  HG172.B84R93 2005
  332.6'092—dc22   2005008904

Ferguson books are available at special discounts when purchased in bulk quantities for businesses, associations, institutions, or sales promotions. Please call our Special Sales Department in New York at (212) 967-8800 or (800) 322-8755.

You can find Ferguson on the World Wide Web at http://www.fergpubco.com

Text design by David Strelecky

Pages 109–120 adapted from Ferguson's *Encyclopedia of Careers and Vocational Guidance, Thirteenth Edition*

Printed in the United States of America

MP JT 10 9 8 7 6 5 4 3 2 1

This book is printed on acid-free paper.

CONTENTS

1

A MIND FOR MONEY

In June 1943, a 13-year-old named Warren Buffett and two of his pals ran away from their homes in Washington, D.C. Hitchhiking, they headed for Hershey, Pennsylvania, where they thought they could get work as caddies at a golf course. That evening they checked into a room in a Hershey inn. The next morning they were questioned by some curious policemen. The boys gave answers that were good enough to send the police away, but they also decided to head back home.

Warren's father was serving his first term as a U.S. Congressman from Omaha, Nebraska. When the Buffett family moved to Washington in January, Warren had been allowed to stay in Omaha with his grandfather and aunt while he finished eighth grade. Now, over the past year, he had completed ninth grade in Washington's Alice Deal Junior High. He had been anything but happy living in

Warren Buffett is one of the world's most successful investors.
(Time Life Pictures/Getty Images)

Washington, however, and his marks in school had been anything but the grades he was capable of. Yet, over the year, he had built up a good business delivering a morning newspaper, *The Washington Post*.

Warren's father then gave his son a challenge: Warren could either improve his grades or quit delivering papers.

Warren liked making money. Within a few months, his work in school improved and he expanded his business to cover five newspaper routes and to include the *Times-Herald*, for customers who did not want the *Post*. By 1945, he was making $175 a month, equal to the full-time pay of many adult wage that year. In the summer, when he and his family visited Omaha while Congress was not in session, the 14-year-old looked over 40 acres of Nebraska farmland. Spending $1,200 from the savings from his newspaper route, he bought the acreage and began collecting rent from a tenant farmer. Thus started the career of one of the world's most successful financiers and investors.

Long-Time Americans Who Went West

Warren Edward Buffett was born in Omaha on August 30, 1930. His ancestors on his father's side had been French Huguenots who came to America in the 1600s. They had been farmers in the area of Huntington, Long Island, for more than 150 years when one of them, Sidney Homan

Buffett, decided to look for a new life out west. It was 1867, just after the end of the Civil War, and the United States was fast stretching westward. Sidney reached the pioneer city of Omaha, a group of log buildings sitting beside the Missouri River and looking across the Great Plains. There he first worked as a stagecoach driver. Then he opened the S. H. Buffett grocery store.

Only three months earlier, the railroad linking east and west had been completed. Omaha was prospering, and the S. H. Buffett grocery grew with the city. By the 1870s, new Omaha settlers, travelers heading west, and railroad men coming and going in both directions all found a bustling city that boasted large cast-iron buildings and even an opera house. All those people had to eat, and S. H. Buffett supplied their hotels, restaurants, and homes with everything from flour and sugar to quail and prairie chickens.

By 1900, Omaha was a city of 140,000 people. Sidney Buffett had not only built a much larger store but had married and produced two sons to join the business. In 1915, one son, Ernest, opened a second store, Buffett & Son, on the city's growing west side, where Omaha's well-to-do were developing pleasant suburban neighborhoods.

Ernest married and had a son named Howard who, when he grew old enough to consider the family business, had a mind of his own. It did not include selling groceries. As a student at the University of Nebraska in Lincoln, he discovered journalism and became editor of the *Daily Nebraskan*. There he met a country girl named Leila Stahl, whose father owned a weekly newspaper in the small town of West Point, Nebraska. At 16, Leila had just graduated from high school and was looking for a newspaper job where she could earn money needed for college. She offered good skills: Since fifth grade she had worked at her father's paper, setting type by hand and on the Linotype machine (that is, a machine that was operated by a keyboard and that created each line of type as a solid piece of metal). She knew how to conduct and write up interviews, and on Thursdays she operated the printing press as it churned out its sheets of newsprint. Howard hired her and fell in love with her.

They were married on December 26, 1925, in the winter after Howard graduated from college. Although he had wanted to work as a newsman, he accepted a job offered by a friend of his father in an insurance company, for his father had paid for college. That job led to another, in which Howard worked for the Union Street Bank as a salesman of securities (that is, certificates of stocks or bonds proving part ownership of a business).

In 1928, Howard and Leila had a daughter whom they named Doris. Warren arrived two years later on an

August day as the stifling 89-degree heat was broken by a cloudburst.

Within a year, just two weeks before Warren's first birthday, his father's bank shut its doors—permanently. The Great Depression, which began in 1929 and which destroyed countless businesses across America, had wiped out Howard Buffett's job and life savings.

Howard came from a long line of determined, thrifty, goal-centered people. He and a partner set up their own business, announcing they had "Investment Securities, Municipal, Corporation and Public Utilities, Stocks and Bonds" for sale. Their income depended on commissions, that is, fees paid as a percentage of the price of whatever they bought or sold for a customer. The commissions were small and infrequent, for Howard and his partner were not well known in the securities business, and Nebraskans, who were suffering from a vast drop in the price of wheat, had little money to invest. Proud farmers, in fact, were humbly accepting free meals in soup kitchens.

At home, Leila Buffett coped with the family's meager income by often going hungry herself so her husband and children could eat full meals. But gradually the family dinner table improved, and the family grew with the arrival of Warren's little sister, Roberta, when he was three. By the time Warren was six, Howard could afford to move his family to a larger home, a roomy brick house on Omaha's North 53rd Street.

Bottle Caps and Golf Balls

Warren had barely started school when his parents began to realize that their son had a mind for money and numbers. As a five-year-old, he set up a stand in front of his home and sold Chiclet chewing gum to whomever passed by. At six, during a family vacation on a lake in Iowa, he discovered he could buy six-packs of Coca-Cola for a quarter. He scurried around the lake selling the Cokes for a nickel each, earning five cents profit per six-pack. Home again in Omaha, he bought bottles of soft drinks from his grandfather's store and spent hot summer evenings going through his neighborhood to sell them at a profit.

When Warren was nine, his mother found him carting home piles of bottle caps from a vending machine in a gas station near his friend Bob Russell's house. He and Bob were counting them to see which brands—root beer, Cokes, or orange drinks—sold the most. At that age, Warren and Bob not only worked as caddies at the Omaha Country Club for $3 a day, they also inspected the edges of the fairways and the nearby "roughs" for abandoned, but usable, golf balls to sell. Warren's mother found baskets of golf balls, sorted by brand name and price, in his bedroom. He organized his friends to sell them and pay him a commission on each sale.

When he was not busy on the golf course, Warren trekked to the Ak-Sar-Ben racetrack (the name was Nebraska spelled backward). There he searched the floors near the betting windows and across the grandstand for torn stubs that were actual winning tickets but had been mistakenly thrown away. The search often paid off for him.

One of Warren's boyhood pastimes was figuring out the symbols for corporate stocks and bonds that were printed on rolls of ticker tape his father brought home from his stock brokerage office. He memorized hundreds. At his father's office, he studied the impressive certificates for stocks and bonds that were mounted on the wall. At the nearby office of stockbrokers Harris Upham, he became a welcome visitor who could be depended on to accurately chalk the current prices of stocks onto the blackboard.

Soon Warren was keeping his own at-home charts showing the ups and downs of various stocks. When he was 11, he decided to buy three shares of an oil company stock, Cities Service Preferred, and three shares for his sister Doris, at $38 per share. Almost immediately, the price dropped to $27 and then rose to $40, whereupon Warren sold the stock. After deducting its sales commission, his father's stock brokerage paid him his first profit in the stock market: $5. And soon after that, Warren learned the value of patience when Cities Service Preferred—the stock he had gotten rid of at $40 per share—shot up to $200 per share.

Warren and his friend Bob Russell spent countless hours giving their brains a workout. Sometimes they kept records of how many times certain letters of the alphabet appeared on a newspaper page. Sometimes they studied an almanac until Bob could quiz Warren with the names of cities and Warren could instantly and accurately tell him their populations. Sometimes Bob asked a question about baseball history and Warren spouted team records or players' batting averages like a major-league statistician. In church on Sunday, Warren's mother quietly observed that her rather docile son was intent on the hymnal, where he found the birth and death years of the composers and could pass the time figuring out just how long each had lived.

Then there was the Russell home, where Warren spent many a happy day and evening. Unlike the Buffetts, who lived on a quiet side street, the Russells dwelt on a main thoroughfare where traffic never seemed to end. "All that traffic," young Warren once said to Mrs. Russell. "What a shame you aren't making money from the people going by."

Warren and Bob Russell studied the mathematics of odds-making, which explores whether one thing is more likely than another to happen. Soon they developed a system for giving tips to people who were betting on horse races. After trying out their system at the Ak-Sar-Ben racetrack and finding that they could make money at the betting windows, they hand-printed sheets with the title *Stable-Boy Selections* that listed their picks for coming races. The boys were busily selling the sheets when racetrack authorities let them know they needed a license to sell them but were too young to get a license.

Move to Washington, D.C.

The year 1942 brought a major change in Warren's life. The bombing of Pearl Harbor by the Japanese on December 7, 1941, had brought the United States into World War II. Democratic President Franklin Delano Roosevelt was so popular that he had been elected in 1940 to a third term. Now the Republicans in Omaha were desperate to find someone who could beat a Democratic candidate for Congress. They nominated the Omaha businessman Howard Buffett, whose strong opinions against Roosevelt's New Deal program were well known.

Few people, including Warren's father himself, expected him to win, but win he did. Twelve-year-old Warren had to pack up his favorite possessions, say good-bye to a throng of good friends who always enjoyed hanging out with him, and move with his family to Washington, D.C. With

Warren's father, a Republican U.S. Congressman, was a strong opponent of the New Deal policies of Democratic president Franklin D. Roosevelt (pictured above). (Getty Images)

the capital city overcrowded in wartime, the Buffetts had to rent a home in Fredericksburg, Virginia, 50 miles outside of downtown Washington.

Now Warren's father, whom he had always been closer to than his mother, was living in a Washington hotel room and coming home only on weekends. Warren was desperately homesick for Omaha. He described his misery in a letter to his Grandpa Ernest. In return he received a letter inviting him to live with his grandfather and his Aunt Alice while he completed the eighth grade. Warren's parents approved.

Back in Omaha, Warren was reunited with his pals and spent the last four months of eighth grade riding his bike all over the city's western neighborhoods. After school hours and on Saturdays, Grandpa Ernest put him to work at Buffett & Sons, where Warren soon learned how a successful business was run. He stocked shelves, heaved heavy crates, and cleaned out vegetable and fruit bins—a chore he especially disliked, for he hated even the smell of groceries. But he liked the activity of rolling the ladder along the wall and climbing up to fetch cans and boxes from the shelves for customers, finding that in a successful business the word *busy* was key. Everybody, he realized, was busy from when the doors opened in the morning until they were locked up at night.

On school days, Warren frequently had lunch at the home of his father's business partner, Carl Falk. There one day he told Mrs. Falk he expected to be a millionaire before he was 30. "Warren," she replied, "why this drive to make so much money?"

"It's not that I *want* money," said her 13-year-old guest. "It's the fun of making money and watching it grow."

2

FROM GOLF COURSE TO GRADUATE SCHOOL

In September 1943, Warren said goodbye to his beloved Grandpa Ernest and Aunt Alice and returned to Washington, D.C., to begin ninth grade at Alice Deal Junior High School. His parents had now moved to 49th Street, just off Massachusetts Avenue in the city's northwest district.

Eager as always to earn money, Warren became a paperboy for *The Washington Post*, getting up early every morning to deliver his papers before school. However, he was not happy. He did not like living in Washington. Younger than most of his schoolmates because he had skipped an earlier grade in Omaha, he had few friends. As the school year went by, the school principal warned Warren's mother that her messy-looking son should improve his appearance. By June, Warren Buffett was an angry 13-year-old ready to revolt against everything and everybody.

That was when Warren and two of his few friends hit the road for Hershey and the golf course where Warren was sure they could be caddies. The police interview the morning after their arrival ended that notion, and, when they got home, a fatherly but firm warning from the congressman—improve school grades or quit delivering papers—subdued Warren's rebellious attitude. He was determined not to give up his paper route.

That fall, teachers found Warren Buffett getting his work done on time and correctly. At *The Washington Post*, circulation managers signed up the 14-year-old to handle more and more papers. Soon he had five routes, delivering some 500 papers each morning. In typical apartment houses—some as tall as eight stories—he took the elevator to a floor half way up, deposited half the building's total papers in the hallway to await him, rose to the top floor, then raced on foot down the stairs, dropping papers at the doors of subscribers.

The *Post* had a competitor, the morning *Times-Herald*. Warren signed up to deliver it along his *Post* routes. If a *Post* subscriber asked him to stop deliveries, he could usually get the customer to start taking the *Times-Herald*, and vice versa. And while he was at it, he peddled magazine subscriptions to his newspaper customers. By summertime 1945, he was making $175 a month.

In November 1944, Congressman Buffett was elected to a second term and Warren was a 10th grader at Washington's Woodrow Wilson High School. He was making friends, playing golf on the school team, and enlisting pals to find, clean up, and sell lost golf balls. One good friend, Donald Danly, who often played the piano while Warren strummed the ukulele, was as crazy as Warren about numbers. They spent hours figuring the odds on certain poker hands or challenging each other to calculate, without pencil and paper, the sums of random double-digit numbers.

Pinball Machines and Tennis Shoes

Donald knew how to fix things. In 1946, during the autumn of their senior year, he bought an old pinball machine for $25 and made it work. He and Warren played it again and again, and it broke again and again. Seeing how easily Donald repaired it, Warren suggested they rent it out in a nearby barbershop.

The barber said he would let the machine in if he got half the proceeds. In the first day, it produced $14. Within little more than a month, the boys had machines in seven barbershops and were making $50 a week under the business title (named for their school) Wilson Coin Operated Machine Company. Warren bought used machines for $25 to $75 each, and Donald raced in his 1938 Buick to any barber who called to say his machine had broken down. Meantime, the boys pretended they were just employees of a larger business. As Warren said years later, "The barbershop operators were always pushing us to put in new machines, and we'd always tell them we'd take it up with the boss. We pretended like we were these hired hands that were carrying machines around and counting money."

Years later, friends from high school days remembered a distinguishing fact about Warren Buffett. "The one thing we used to joke about," recalled one, "he didn't wear anything other than tennis shoes. Even in the dead of winter."

"We used to get a kick out of Warren and his sneakers," said another. "He used to wear 'em year-round. I don't care if the snow was a foot deep, he had sneakers on."

At home, 16-year-old Warren continued to be devoted to his father, who had been elected in November 1946 to his third two-year term as a Nebraska representative in the U.S. Congress. He knew his father's extremely conservative position on almost any issue. Warren was also aware that, when Congress raised its own salaries from $10,000 to $12,500 during his father's first term, Howard Buffett had firmly declared that he had been hired to represent Nebraska at $10,000 and that was all the pay he would take.

Now came the question of college. The congressman suggested that Warren apply for admission to the University of Pennsylvania's Wharton School of Finance and Commerce. Warren said he did not need that. He had earned more than $5,000 (an amount roughly equal to $45,000 in the year 2005) delivering some 600,000 news-papers. Wilson Coin Operated Machines and 40 acres of Nebraska farmland were both producing steady income. And he had already read every word of more than 100 books on business. What could Wharton or any other business college teach him?

Howard Buffett reminded his son that he would be graduating from high school almost three months before he turned 17. Reluctantly, Warren agreed to give Wharton a try.

At the Woodrow Wilson High School graduation in June 1947, Warren Buffett stood 16th in a class of 374. The caption under his photo in the Wilson yearbook said, "Likes math. A future stockbroker." The girlfriend of Warren's friend Donald Danly asked him if he expected to make a career in Washington. "No," he said. "I'm going to live in Omaha."

Romping in a Rolls Royce

At Wharton, Warren Buffett soon found out he was right: No professor seemed to know as much about his subject as Warren already knew. When he visited Omaha during a holiday, Mary Falk, wife of his father's business partner, asked him if he was studying hard. "All I need to do," he said, "is open the book the night before and drink a big bottle of Pepsi-Cola and I'll make 100."

At home in Washington for the summer after his first year at Wharton, Warren was ready to quit school. His father persuaded him to return for a second year. Meantime, Warren cavorted around the nation's capital with his friend Donald Danly in a 1928 Rolls Royce automobile that Donald had bought in a junkyard, painted dark blue, and fixed up to run. Their favorite "act" was to drive downtown with Donald dressed as a chauffeur while his girlfriend and Warren posed in the back seat as a wealthy couple. On cue, Donald stalled the engine, opened the hood, and vainly tried to start the car until a small crowd gathered. Then a haughty Warren rapped the windshield with his cane and pointed to the presumed trouble spot, which Donald pretended to repair, and away the trio drove.

Back at Wharton, Warren lived at his fraternity house, Alpha Sigma Phi, where his college brothers found he played a challenging game of bridge. He could be counted on to express his opinions in lively, entertaining conversations. "He was a very funny kid," one later said, "very clever. It wasn't boffo slapstick, it was dry. When he was on, he was fun—a lot of laughs."

At fraternity-house beer parties on weekends, the brothers liked to crowd around Warren (who, unlike the beer drinkers, consumed only Pepsi-Cola) with their visiting dates and listen to his astute answers to long strings of questions about politics and economics. Those who sat in classrooms with him sensed his superiority over graduate students who were delivering boring lectures. "Warren came to the conclusion," said one, "that there wasn't anything Wharton could teach him. And he was right."

In November 1948, Howard Buffett ran for re-election to Congress and lost. He moved his wife and daughters back to Omaha. When Warren finished his second year at Wharton in June 1949, he transferred to the University of Nebraska at Lincoln. He never looked back. "I didn't feel I was learning that much," he said later. "Nebraska called, Wharton repelled."

Fifty Paperboys and 2,640 Golf Balls

With the two Wharton years on his record, Warren set out to earn his bachelor's degree in three years rather than the usual four. In the fall semester 1949, he took on five courses—almost all in economics and business—then scheduled six in the spring of 1950. At the same time, he tackled a busy job at the *Lincoln Journal*. He was the supervisor of some 50 boys who delivered the newspaper in six of southeastern Nebraska's rural counties. His work, for 75 cents an hour, involved driving around the territory late in the afternoon or early in the evening to line up new delivery boys as fast as old ones quit.

In the winter of 1950, Warren decided it was time to start up his golf-ball business again. He made his Wharton chum Jerry Orans his sales agent in Philadelphia, shipping him the cleaned-up balls. By July, he had earned $1,200 by selling 2,640 balls. At the end of the summer, when he had moved home and taken three more courses on the University of Nebraska's Omaha campus to earn his degree, he had a total of $9,800 in savings from handling newsboys and selling golf balls.

Now he sent in an application to the Harvard Graduate School of Business Administration. An alumnus in Chicago invited the 19-year-old applicant there for an interview. It lasted only 10 minutes. "Those stuffed shirts at Harvard," Warren later said, "decided 19 was too young to get admitted and advised me to wait a year or two."

Warren Buffett was not waiting. He applied to the Columbia University Graduate School of Business in New York. A Columbia professor named Benjamin Graham had written a book, The Intelligent Investor, that Warren admired. Professor Graham had no way of knowing that he was soon to become the most valuable lifelong mentor of an eager 19-year-old who was headed his way.

3

THE INTELLIGENT INVESTOR

The title of Benjamin Graham's book *The Intelligent Investor* described exactly what Warren Buffett wanted to be. He had thought and thought about investors—people who buy shares of ownership in businesses in hopes that they will be so profitable that the businesses can repay them more money than they invested in them. He liked Graham's basic advice, which urged the intelligent investor to pay no attention to the trends that Wall Street investors typically follow. Rather, said Graham in his book, the investor should look for companies whose stocks could be bought for much less than their actual value.

Finding such companies, Graham wrote, was not easy. It took plenty of patience, for the investor had to carefully examine every aspect of a company that was being considered: its assets, its earnings (that is, the money it had left after paying for costs and expenses), and its expectations for the future. By analyzing such information, the investor could figure out the *intrinsic value* of shares in the company (a value that had nothing to do with how shares were priced in the stock market).

Stock-market prices, according to Graham, were like a popularity contest. They showed how investors were reacting emotionally to the company. Rumor and hearsay, rather than facts, often affected prices on the stock market, and such prices seldom reflected the true worth of the company.

Graham's conclusion was that the intelligent investor should buy stock when its price stood well below the stock's intrinsic value or true worth. Then the investor should stand back and wait patiently for the stock market to catch on as, sooner or later, it almost always did.

In essence, that point of view was what Warren Buffett got from reading Graham's book. He liked what he had read. In his father's office in Omaha and in stockbrokers' offices in Philadelphia while he was at Wharton, he had followed tips on stocks. He had seen the fortunes of stock speculators (people who buy or sell stocks in the expectation that their prices will go up or down) rise and fall with the market. He had never thought that such systems, which really were not systems at all, made much sense.

The book The Intelligent Investor *by Benjamin Graham (pictured above) had an enormous impact on Warren's developing career.* (Associated Press)

At Columbia in September 1950, Warren was one of 20 students in Graham's classroom. He was charmed by the professor's way of not giving absolute approval or disapproval to a student's answer to a question. "That's interesting," Graham would muse. "What line of thought brought you to that conclusion?"

Professor Graham showed his students how to read a company's annual report and financial statement in detail to deduce the firm's intrinsic value. He had them study the balance sheets of two quite different-looking companies and then revealed that both were from the airplane maker Boeing—but at different times in its history. In effect, Graham was teaching Warren and his classmates to study what a company revealed about itself in its printed information. From all that was published, they could determine the intrinsic value of the company.

Warren ate it up. "He had all the answers," said one classmate later. "He was raising his hand, he was leading the discussions. He had tremendous enthusiasm. He always had more to say than anyone else."

Finding Out about GEICO

Intrigued by his professor's knowledge and attitude, Warren wanted to know more about him. During Warren's second semester at Columbia, he learned that Graham was chairman of GEICO, the Government Employees

Insurance Company, which was headquartered in Washington, D.C.

In November 1950 Howard Buffett had been re-elected to Congress after his two years out of office. Thus, in the spring of 1951 Warren headed for a weekend visit with his folks. When he got off the train in Washington on Saturday morning, however, he first went to GEICO's office at 15th and K Streets. There a janitor responded to his pounding on the locked door. As Warren insisted he wanted to talk to somebody, he was escorted to the only other employee in the building, GEICO's financial vice president, Lorimer Davidson, who suddenly faced a barrage of questions from a young stranger.

"After we talked for fifteen minutes," Davidson later said, "I knew I was talking to an extraordinary man. He asked searching and highly intelligent questions. What was GEICO? What was its method of doing business, its outlook, its growth potential? He asked the type of questions that a good security analyst would ask. He was trying to find out what I knew."

Their conversation lasted four hours. Warren learned that GEICO had been the brainchild of a Texan who thought of selling automobile insurance by direct mail to government employees, who filed fewer claims than other groups. Direct selling meant there were no agents who had to be paid. With fewer claims and no agents, costs were lower than in other insurance companies. And insurance was a solid business because money in payment of premiums was always coming in. Called the *float,* this money could be held and invested to earn more money until some of it was needed to pay claims.

Warren went back to New York intrigued with GEICO. Digging for facts, he learned that the company regularly made five times as much profit as other insurance companies. Yet stock-market experts on insurance companies insisted that the price of stock in GEICO was too high, so stockbrokers just did not recommend it to the clients they advised. Warren Buffett found that hard to understand.

Omaha and Matrimony

In 22 years of teaching at Columbia, Professor Ben Graham had never given any student an A +, but that was the final mark he awarded Warren Buffett as he graduated with his master's degree in economics in June 1951. Upon graduating, Warren offered to go to work for Graham—for no pay whatsoever—in a small mutual fund the professor managed. Graham advised him not to work in Wall Street.

Warren headed back to Omaha and soon went to work in his father's brokerage firm, Buffett-Falk & Co. A friend asked if the firm would become known as Buffett & Son.

"No," said a mischievous Warren, "Buffett & Father."

Following his year at Columbia, Warren still had the $9,800 he had earned delivering newspapers, running the pinball-machine business, and selling reconditioned golf balls. Now, using Buffett-Falk as his broker and putting to work the study skills Ben Graham had taught him, he began carefully analyzing unknown companies and buying shares in them.

During that summer of 1951, his mind was not only on making prudent investments. It was also on an Omaha girl who had roomed with his sister Roberta at Northwestern University. Her father was well known both as a professor of psychology and as a minister, and he had managed one of Howard Buffett's campaigns for Congress. The girl's name was Susan Thompson. Known as Susie, she had a twinkling smile and a ready warmth that reached out and embraced strangers as well as friends.

Warren was in love. So was Susie—but not with him. She had a steady boyfriend from high school and her Northwestern days. She watched, as she later recalled, as Warren "went over to my parents' home every night and played the ukulele. My father played the mandolin since he was 20, so he was really excited about having someone to play with. So Warren did that every night, while I went out with this other person."

After several weeks, Susie broke off with her boyfriend and began going on dates with Warren. She discovered—and liked—his outrageous sense of humor. She accepted his equally outrageous eating and drinking preferences: Pepsi-Cola morning, noon, and night, with meals and between meals, and hamburgers whenever and wherever possible.

On Saturday, April 19, 1952, family and friends gathered in the Dundee Presbyterian Church for Susie and Warren's wedding. The bride was 19; the groom was 21. Looking back years later, Warren said that until he met Susie he had been lonely.

Taking a commission on selling stocks and bonds at his father's brokerage firm was not Warren's idea of how to earn money. The salesman's task of convincing customers to invest was, for him, an uncomfortable chore. He was still itching to work for his Columbia mentor, Ben Graham, whose firm specialized in finding stocks priced so low that, because their futures were promising, there was no risk in buying them.

Warren knew how uncomfortable he was in dealing with customers, and he had a strong fear of speaking in public. To help overcome both problems, he took a course in public speaking offered by Dale Carnegie & Associates, a service that taught business executives and others how to be successful. It had been founded by Dale Carnegie, author of the book *How to Win Friends and Influence People*, which had sold millions of copies since its publication in

1936. Among Carnegie's best-known rules were "Believe that you will succeed, and you will," and "Learn to love, respect and enjoy other people." They were rules that Warren Buffett was already living by.

After taking the speaking course, Warren taught a night class on investment principles at the University of Omaha. It gave him a chance not only to practice his speaking skills but to let his thirtyish and fortyish students (many of them doctors) in on Ben Graham's ideas.

Warren with his daughter (left) and wife (right), both named Susie, in 1997 (Corbis)

Warren and Susie Buffett's first home was a three-room apartment they rented in Omaha for $65 a month. Included for the low price was a family of mice. The Buffetts soon found that the mice liked to explore their shoes at night. When their daughter, whom they named Susie, arrived in 1953, they saved money by turning a dresser drawer into a bassinet for her.

With Ben Graham in New York

One day in 1954, Warren answered his phone at Buffett-Falk to hear Ben Graham's voice asking him if he still wanted to work for the professor's mutual fund. Warren booked the next flight he could get to New York.

At Graham-Newman Corp., Warren Buffett joined five other employees in a small office in the Chanin Building on East 42nd Street. His job was to look for stocks that could be bought at absurdly low prices and report to Graham on what he found. Graham then decided—immediately—whether to buy the stock.

Working for Graham, Warren began to realize that he himself was developing a viewpoint on stock buying that was different from his boss's. Graham wanted only numbers—the facts about a company that could be found in such sources as Standard & Poor's, a research company that, since 1860, has provided all kinds of financial information on more than a thousand corporations. Warren, however, wanted to know how a company worked, why it was better than its competition, whose brains made it a likely future leader among corporations.

Sometimes the professor looked at the numbers and did not buy, but Warren did. For example, he discovered that stock in Union Street Railway of New Bedford, Massachusetts, was available and priced at $45 a share, yet the company was sitting on a supply of cash that was equal to $120 a share. In effect, this meant that a share was worth almost three times as much as the price at which it was for sale. When Graham said he would not buy Union Street Railway, Warren bought shares for himself.

Susie, Warren, and little Susie were living in a rented garden apartment in White Plains, a suburb of New York City. From there Warren commuted to Grand Central Terminal, a short walk from his office. In 1954, the Buffetts welcomed their second child, Howard Graham Buffett. This time, the bassinet was not a dresser drawer. Rather, Warren borrowed a crib for the baby boy.

By 1956, Ben Graham was ready to close up his mutual fund and retire to a teaching job at the University of California at Los Angeles, and Warren and Susie were ready to move back to Omaha. Warren's quiet investments over five and a half years had grown his personal capital from the $9,800 he had just after college to $140,000. This meant, he was certain, that he could launch his own business and never again work for somebody else. The business would not be like a stock brokerage firm, in which the stockbroker advises the investor and handles the details of buying or selling the stocks after the investor makes the decision. Rather, it would be one in which he took full charge of investing other people's money for them.

In Omaha, Warren and Susie rented a house two blocks from the Buffett & Son store. On May 1, 1956, seven people—some family, some friends—signed papers making them partners in Buffett Associates, Ltd.

4

$7 MILLION IN 10 YEARS

The seven people who joined Warren in Buffett Associates were called limited partners. They each put in $105,000. Warren himself was the general partner. He put in only $100. But he had all the responsibility for investing the money wisely so it produced profits for them. This was to be his full-time job as he worked from a simple office: his bedroom.

Here is how the partnership worked: If Buffett's investments made any profit up to 4 percent, the limited partners could keep all of it. If the profit was more than 4 percent, however, Warren could keep 25 percent of that additional profit, with the partners getting the other 75 percent. In effect, he was taking the risk that, if the investments he made did not produce at least 4 percent profit, he would earn nothing.

In August, the stockholders of the Graham-Newman Corp., including Warren Buffett, met in New York. As expected, they voted to end the corporation, for none of them believed it could survive without Ben Graham. "Graham-Newman can't continue," said one who headed a New York stock brokerage firm, "because the only guy they have to run it is this kid named Warren Buffett. And who'd want to ride with him?"

Becoming a Millionaire at 32

By the end of 1956, the 26-year-old "kid named Warren Buffett" was managing some $300,000 in capital (roughly equal to $2.7 million in 2005). For $31,500, he and Susie bought a five-bedroom house that they lovingly named "Buffett's Folly." There he set aside one room as his office. In 1958, their son Peter joined the family.

By 1961, the number of limited partners in Buffett Associates grew from the original seven to 90. They included friends, neighbors, former fellow students, and friends of friends all across America. A group of 11 doctors each invested $10,000. Some individuals put in as much as $100,000 each. All accepted Warren's rules: They could not ask and would not know just where he invested their money, and they could put more money in or take their money out on only one day—December 31—each year. In effect, each partner was saying, "Take my money.

Invest it in any way you think best. I won't ask you what you did with it. And I'll wait until the last day of the year to give you more to invest or to get any profit you make for me."

In 1958, Warren read a best-selling book that reinforced the buy-and-hold strategy he had learned from Ben Graham. It was *Common Stocks and Uncommon Profits* by Philip A. Fisher. "From him," Warren later said, "I learned the value of the 'scuttlebutt' approach: Go out and talk to competitors, suppliers and customers to find out how an industry or a company really operates." He used this dig-in-and-find-out method as he bought stock in 41 different companies, ranging from a mapmaker to a manufacturer of windmills and farm implements to a little-known insurance company.

How did Warren and his partners judge how well he was doing? The standard reporting system in the world of financial investing is the Dow Jones Industrial Average (often called simply *the Dow*). Looking at 30 prominent industrial firms, it computes the average price of their common stocks for each hour of every business day. Warren's primary goal was always to do better than the Dow. Over the five years from 1957 through 1961, in fact, he did just that: Buffett Associates grew by 251 percent, while the Dow went up by 74.3 percent. At the start of 1962, the total worth of Buffett

Associates was $7.2 million. Of that, $1 million was Buffett's own. He was 32 years old.

Annual Reports, Cheeseburgers, Golf, and Bridge

Warren was now ready to grow some more. He set up a new firm, Buffett Partnerships, Ltd., and merged the partners from Buffett Associates into it. But he added a tougher rule: Now a new partner had to start with an investment of not less than $100,000. Warren also moved his desk from his home office to an office building on Kiewit Plaza on the edge of Omaha's business area. There he allowed himself the luxury of a secretary to handle correspondence and routine phone calls and an administrative assistant to take care of the ordinary business details of running Buffett Partnerships. And there Warren spent long days devoted to studying business magazines and corporate annual reports, usually lunching alone on cheeseburgers and French fries (preferably from McDonald's) and Pepsi-Cola.

While he spent long hours alone in his office looking and looking for stocks to buy that fit his particular rules, Warren Buffett was not a loner. He had buddies on the golf course, where he was admired for the concentration with which he played the game. Other pals met with him regularly to play bridge (he always brought along plenty of

Pepsi-Cola), a game in which he was a tough competitor. All found him an enjoyable source of stories and jokes—a guy who was fun to be with. But all his wide circle of friends, whether investors or bridge buddies or golfers, knew there was no point in asking Warren for advice on their own investments or trying to find out just where he was investing the money of Buffett partners. He gave stock tips to no one.

A typical stock he would not talk about was one that Warren started buying in 1962. Like the Union Street Railway stock he had bought while working for Ben Graham, it was a bargain. It was also, by coincidence, located in New Bedford, Massachusetts, where textile mills were rapidly dying. This one, called Berkshire Hathaway Inc., made linings for men's suits, a product for which there was less and less demand and which was being made more cheaply in Asia and down south in America. But Berkshire Hathaway stock was selling for only $7.60 a share while the company held double that—$16.50 a share—in working capital. Like Union Street Railway, that was Warren Buffett's kind of bargain. Knowing the shares were worth twice their asking price, he quietly began buying Berkshire Hathaway stock for his partnership.

In that same year, 1962, a man named Charlie Munger moved home to Omaha from California. A lawyer six years older than Warren, he was known for his brilliance, strong opinions on almost all subjects, and tough com- mon-sense ethics. He and Warren had met in 1959 and had become close friends by telephone. The more they talked, the more they advised each other, for it was obvi- ous they thought alike on business subjects. Munger had even developed his own investment partnership in California. Now Charlie Munger moved into the offices of the Buffett Partnership as Warren's partner.

In effect, while Charlie Munger became Warren's only real partner in the true sense of the word, he also became his mentor. Munger encouraged Warren to think not just about the inexpensive stock of companies that had hidden value but to look for those that, whatever their current stock price, were sure to grow significantly. Commenting later on, Warren said, "Charlie kept pushing me back to the idea that what we really needed to own was the won- derful business."

In 1962, those who had bought Buffett partnerships began to receive letters twice a year from Warren Buffett. His letters filled them in on his approach to investing and were so well written and entertaining—often including funny if not absurd comments—that Warren's investors looked forward to them.

"I believe in establishing yardsticks prior to the act," he said in his first letter, "retrospectively, almost anything

Charlie Munger (left) and Warren address journalists at a Berkshire Hathaway shareholders meeting. (Associated Press)

can be made to look good in relation to something or other." The yardstick he applied, he added, was the Dow. He intended to do better than the Dow by an average of 10 points (points are used to quote or describe stock-market prices; one point is equal to one dollar).

"Tell us how he *made* it."

At this time, in 1963, Warren noticed a different kind of company that fascinated him. It had no factories and made no products, yet a million people carried it in their wallets and purses. It was, in fact, a revolutionary idea: the charge card. Its name was American Express. For almost 100 years, American Express had been the world leader in traveler's checks, but the charge-card idea was only five years old.

Warren watched the price of stock in American Express drop from $60 in October 1963 to $35 by early 1964. He knew that Wall Street stockbrokers were advising their clients that American Express had had some difficulties and they should sell their shares as soon as they could.

Thinking for himself and paying no attention to rumors, Warren put his "scuttlebutt" approach to work. He got into his Volkswagen Beetle and drove around Omaha to his favorite restaurants. At each, he lingered near the cash register and watched as customer after customer used the American Express card to pay the check. Next he stopped in at travel agencies and saw the same thing. At banks he found that eight out of 10 traveler's checks they sold bore the American Express imprint.

As usual under the rules of the Buffett Partnership, Warren did not tell his investors what he was doing. None of them knew it as he spent nearly one fourth of the partnership's wealth to buy shares of American Express on their behalf. Using the Ben Graham philosophy of looking for intrinsic value, he had noticed, analyzed, and bought a stock that was sure to regain its position and grow far beyond it. And by the end of 1964, when the partnership had grown 28 percent larger, he knew he was right. Its assets, including the American Express stock (the price of which had gone back up), were $22 million and Warren's own net worth was just under $4 million.

Warren's family and friends knew, and talked about, how being a millionaire with plenty of money really meant nothing to him. What mattered was *making* the money. He and Susie stayed in their original grey stucco house on a busy street, adding only one luxury: a racquetball court. When he realized his Volkswagen was perhaps too modest for escorting partnership visitors from the airport, he asked Susie to go buy any car. He did not care what kind she bought, as long as it made a better impression. She bought a Cadillac.

Warren's kids got a good example of their father's viewpoint on money when he and Susie took them, during a vacation trip, to see San Simeon, the California mansion of William Randolph Hearst. Newspaper publisher Hearst had made his fortune several times over and spent at least one fortune on this extravagant home. As members of a group tour moving through the house, the Buffett family heard the tour guide recite the price Hearst had paid for each painting, each carpet, each antique desk or table or chair. Finally, the group heard an exasperated Warren calling out from their midst, "Don't tell us how he spent it. Tell us how he *made* it."

By the mid-1960s, as America struggled through bitter battles over civil rights, Warren was changing his mind about some things. Much as he loved his father, he could no longer agree with the former Congressman's ultra conservative viewpoints. Howard Buffett, who was a strong member of the right-wing John Birch Society, believed the less government the better. Warren, on the other hand, thought strong government was not only a necessity but was essential to the protection of the civil rights of citizens. He resigned from the Omaha Rotary Club, declaring he could not agree with its racist policies. He switched his voter registration from the Republican to the Democratic Party.

Soon afterward, in the spring of 1964, Howard Buffett died. Warren mourned quietly, keeping fond memories of his dad to himself, but others knew he had lost his best friend.

Putting Berkshire Hathaway to Work

By 1965, Berkshire Hathaway, the company that made suit linings, had turned around and was no longer losing money. Warren Buffett had the partnership spend $11 million to buy 49 percent of the stock, giving him (in effect) control of the company at a cost of $15 a share. On Wall Street, the price immediately rose to $18 a share.

Now Warren put Berkshire's strong pile of capital to work. Using what he had learned about the insurance business from studying GEICO, he checked out Omaha's National Indemnity Company and found that its stock was worth $50 a share but was selling for $33 a share. He had Berkshire Hathaway spend $8.6 million of its capital to buy National Indemnity outright. This gave Berkshire the benefit of the insurance company's float, which was a steady stream of cash that could be invested. Warren himself had a unique definition of float, saying it was "money we have but don't own." The cash flow gave Berkshire the money to make profitable investments, including buying a string of weekly newspapers in the Omaha area and a major bank in Rockford, Illinois.

Usually when a company is bought the new owners get rid of the former owners, bringing in new executives of their own. Warren Buffett did no such thing. He did not want to run the companies he (that is, Berkshire Hathaway) bought. He wanted the former owners on the job running them. After all, he was buying them because they were run well. His point of view astonished employees and executives alike.

The year 1966 marked the 10th anniversary of Warren's partnership business. By then Berkshire Hathaway owned 5 percent of Walt Disney Productions at a cost of $4 million. Altogether, Berkshire could count up total assets of $44 million. Over 10 years, it had grown 1,156 percent, while the Dow had grown 122.9 percent. And Warren

Buffett was writing, in his January 1966 letter to his partners, "Susie and I have an investment of $6,849,936, which should keep me from slipping away to the movies in the afternoon." In other words, 35-year-old Warren Buffett was a millionaire almost seven times over and was paying strict attention to the business of making money.

5

WASHINGTON, BUFFALO, AND SAN FRANCISCO

Over the next several years, the United States was fully engaged in the Vietnam War in Asia, a fact that contributed to economic growth at home. Wall Street enjoyed a bull market—a time when stock prices keep rising. The Buffett Partnership gained $40 million—an increase of 59 percent in value—in 1968 alone, reaching $104 million in assets. This achievement was 50 percent better than the Dow's rise at the same time. But Warren Buffett was not happy.

He explained his unhappiness in a letter to his partners in May 1969, saying he was "unable to find any bargains in the current market." Therefore, he said, he would quit. He would liquidate—that is, sell or convert into cash—all the partnership's assets except two: Berkshire Hathaway and Diversified Retailing, a company that owned a chain of dress shops.

It took a year to sell off the dozens of blocks of stock the partnership had amassed. Warren offered each partner his or her share either in cash or in stock in Berkshire or Diversified. He translated his own share into the two, resulting in his owning 29 percent of Berkshire Hathaway. As Berkshire's largest shareholder by far, he then became chairman of its board of directors.

Warren's partners were quite satisfied. Anyone who had put in $10,000 in 1957 gained a profit of $150,270 over the 13 years, while anyone watching $10,000 in the Dow over the same period saw it rise only to $15,260. In percentages, the Buffett Partnership rose 29.5 percent and the Dow only 7.4 percent. Those who paid attention to such results did not hesitate to take most of their partnership profits in Berkshire stock instead of cash. Warren advised them not to think of Berkshire as a stock anymore but rather as a business investing in other businesses.

Family Life and Chocolate Investments

As Warren's three children grew into teenagers, they sensed their father's enormous powers of concentration. Susie saw it when, on the very day she got her driver's license, she had to tell her father she had dented his car. He did not look up from his reading, simply asking, "Was anyone hurt?" When she said no, he kept on reading. A while later he said, "Suz, remember, the other guy is a jerk." And when she wanted to use the car that evening, he handed her the keys without hesitation.

Friends of Susie, Howard, and Peter Buffett called the Buffett home a "safe house." They knew they could walk in anytime, help themselves to whatever they could find in the refrigerator, and play racquetball uninvited on the Buffett's court out back. "If the snow fell and the city stopped," one of the kids' friends later recalled, "that's where you went. Sitting in the family room was so damned nice. Saturday nights the family room would be full of kids. Mrs. Buffett would be there. We'd be playing our music for her. She'd be playing music for us. Long about twelve-thirty in the morning you'd hear, 'Susan-O, you coming up?' There were never any rules. When he went to bed, we turned down the music."

The teens discovered the California lifestyle in the summer of 1971 after Warren and "Big Susie" bought a vacation home in Laguna Beach, an oceanfront community south of Los Angeles. They counted 13 different teenagers who came to surf and hang out. All were aware that Mr. Buffett welcomed the teens in his home, but that he disappeared every morning with a sheaf of papers as soon as a large envelope arrived from Omaha.

In 1971, a California friend of Warren's phoned to tell him that See's Candy Shops—a West Coast chain that made and sold its own special chocolates—was for sale. The company was asking $30 million. Warren checked on See's, learning that its customers would pay anything to enjoy the special taste of the See's brand. It was the kind of "wonderful business" Charlie Munger had long been trying to get Warren to buy. Through Berkshire Hathaway he offered $25 million in cash. See's accepted. It was by far the largest investment yet made by Berkshire or Buffett.

When he had been unable to find any more bargains in 1969 and 1970, Warren had put money from National Indemnity's float into bonds rather than stocks. (Buying a bond is like making a loan to a company or government, usually to help pay for a building or other construction. The bondholder receives a certificate entitling him or her to payments of interest over a certain period.) By 1972, Berkshire had $84 million in bond certificates and only $17 million in stocks, while Wall Street brokers were rubbing their hands in glee as they rejoiced in the bull market that was sending stock prices to all-time highs.

The next year everything changed. Suddenly the Dow, which had been higher than 1,000, dropped to 950. Stock prices fell to half of what they had been three or four

Warren and his son, Howard, in 2004 (Associated Press)

years earlier. Warren Buffett looked around and saw bargains everywhere. He cashed in bonds as fast as he could and bought the stocks of famous, as well as lesser known, companies—General Motors and U.S. Truck Lines, Ford Motor and realtor Coldwell Banker, discount retail store Vornado and S&H Green Stamp makers Sperry & Hutchinson—a total of 25 in the year 1973.

"Washington society is agog"

Warren's most important buy that year was probably also his most satisfying. In February he noticed that his boyhood paper-route newspaper, *The Washington Post*, was one of the bargains in the stock market, where experts were figuring the Post company was worth $100 million. He got details, finding out that the Post owned not only the mills that made its newsprint (that is, the paper on which it printed the news) but *Newsweek* magazine and four television stations as well. Warren calculated that the Post company had to be worth at least $400 million—four times Wall Street's evaluation. He began buying Post shares, and by October he owned more of *The Washington Post* than anybody except its publisher, Katharine Graham, and her family.

The Post company was not Warren's only newspaper buy. He made Berkshire the largest buyer of stock in the *Boston Globe,* which had no newspaper competition. He also bought stock in several smaller newspapers and news chains, for, by mid-1974, the country was in a major recession, the Dow was down to 607 points, and inflation was increasing. What Warren knew was that any newspaper that was the only one in town could raise its advertising rates to keep up with inflation. Advertisers had to accept the rates or, if they didn't advertise, risk losing customers.

Publisher Katharine Graham, whose family controlled the Post company, soon invited Warren to join its board of directors. He began to visit Washington as often as once a month, advising Graham on ways to improve the profits of her newspaper and her television stations, each of which earned barely 10 percent. He brought piles of annual reports for her to study, teaching her his basic systems of analysis. He urged her to have the Post buy back much of its stock from its shareholders, so that as the company grew it would enjoy larger growth per share (that is, the fewer the shares, the more the growth for each one). He was one of her chief advisers during a bitter four-month-long strike against the newspaper by the pressmen's union, which she won.

Katharine Graham and Warren Buffett became close personal friends. When he visited her at home, Kay (as she was known to her good friends) served his beloved hamburgers, and, for dessert, strawberry ice cream. His simple tastes caught the attention of the capital's gossip columnist, Liz Smith, who commented, "Washington society is agog because Mr. B. drinks Pepsi-Cola with his meals, no matter how chic the gathering."

Susie's New Career and Trouble with GEICO

In 1975, people in Omaha began to notice a new local talent who was drawing crowds to the French Cafe, a restaurant and nightclub in the city's popular cobblestone market area. The attraction was a singer named Susie Buffett, wife of the city's financial wizard. Susie was fulfilling a longtime dream and Warren encouraged her, telling her she'd be sorry later on if she hadn't tried it.

Susie's act was a hit. She played to French Cafe patrons for a six-week run. "Susie was a cabaret singer," a friend later recalled. "I remember seeing Warren there one night. Seeing the expression on his face. He was digging it."

Warren himself said, "When Susie sings, it is so beautiful I can't breathe." One Omaha audience included singer Neil Sedaka, who advised Susie to turn professional. She auditioned and sang in New York nightclubs and signed a contract with William Morris, one of the leading talent agencies.

While Susie was developing her new career, Warren noticed that GEICO was in trouble. He had sold his shares in it when he closed the Buffett Partnerships. Over the years, he had known that it had changed its strategy of insuring only low-risk drivers. Keeping its prices low and taking on higher-risk drivers, it had become a giant among auto insurers. By 1974, its stock was worth $42 a share. But high-risk drivers were filing more claims than expected, new laws that established no-fault insurance meant more claims to be paid, and inflation was raising the costs of repairing injured cars and people. Thus, in 1975, GEICO paid out $126 million more than it took in. The stock dropped to below $5. GEICO was nearly bankrupt—a phrase that meant it was reduced almost to financial ruin.

By July 1976, Warren was studying GEICO's situation in his usual thorough way. He saw that, when compared to other insurance companies, it still had the advantage of operating at extremely low cost, but he also saw that its largest problem was poor management—executives who just did not know how to run the company. That could be fixed. With the share price only slightly higher than $2, he had Berkshire Hathaway buy $4 million worth of GEICO stock.

Warren kept close watch as GEICO's top executives changed, bringing new thinking and raising new money to head off bankruptcy. Within a few months, shares in GEICO were priced above $8 and Berkshire had $23 million invested in the company.

In September 1976, while GEICO was occupying much of his time and thought, Warren had to face the fact that his beloved mentor, Ben Graham, had died at age 82. Speaking years later about Graham's influence on his career, he said, "The best thing I did was to chose the right heroes. It all comes from Graham."

The Paper Boy Buys a Big Paper

Late in December 1976, Warren learned from Kay Graham that she was considering buying the *Buffalo Evening News*. The paper, which was read in a higher percentage of big-city homes than any other U.S. daily, was being sold by its long-time family owners. It was just what Warren had wanted ever since his boyhood: his own newspaper.

Warren did some homework. He learned that the *News* sold more than twice as many papers every day as the city's morning *Buffalo Courier-Express* and that it took in 75 percent more money from advertising than its competitor. He told Kay Graham that if she did not buy it, he probably would.

Kay Graham said no. Warren talked it over with Charlie Munger. They offered the owners $32.5 million—more than they had yet paid for anything. And they faced a bigger challenge than any they had yet met, for this time they were not buying stock in a company, they were buying the company itself. The *Buffalo Evening News* was now Warren's own newspaper.

As chairman of the *News* company, Warren was soon busy with the publisher's usual worries: promotional plans, advertising rates, boosting circulation. He thrived on it, sending a note to his friend Kay Graham: "I'm having so much fun with this it is sinful."

By November, Warren asked the paper's managing editor to plan on publishing a Sunday edition—something the *News* had never done. It had never challenged the position of the *Courier-Express* as Buffalo's big Sunday paper, but now it did.

The *Courier-Express* went to a federal court, charging the *News* with being a monopoly. It said the *News* was trying to put it out of business by selling its Sunday edition at a price lower than other papers in upstate and western New York and by selling seven papers, during a promotion period, for the price of six. In the witness chair as the judge considered whether there was enough evidence to bring about a trial, Warren Buffett was as calm and collected as if he were at home in the family room. When the judge asked him to explain why he thought the Sunday *News* would not outsell the *Courier-Express*, he quietly replied, "Well, you assume that the *Courier* has been publishing for many, many, many years, all alone in the market—that people's habits are very strong. I shave my face on the same side every morning and put on the same shoe first and people are creatures of habit. And the product that they have been receiving every day for a great many years has an enormous advantage."

Only four days before the first Sunday edition of the *News* was to be published, the judge decided it was likely that a trial would prove that the *News*, intending to gain a monopoly over the market for Buffalo newspaper readers, was using unfair tactics. He said it could go ahead with its Sunday edition, but only with limited promotion. "There are only two newspapers now," said his decision. "If the plan works as I find it is intended to work, there will be but one left."

The decision cost the *News* a major loss of advertising dollars, not to mention the loss of both weekday and Sunday readers. But Warren Buffett told his lawyers to appeal to a higher court, even though he knew that appeals often take years to be resolved. And he told his editors to keep working to provide their readers more news, more sports, more everything than *Courier-Express* readers were getting.

Changes on the Home Front

By September of 1977, Susie was appearing regularly at the French Cafe and on other Omaha stages. Young Susie was married and living in California. Howard had dropped out of college and was organizing an excavating business near Omaha. Peter was a student at Stanford University.

Then Susie moved out. She left Omaha, telling her kids and her husband she just had to live on her own. She rented an apartment in San Francisco. But she said she did not want a legal separation. And she and Warren talked on the phone almost every day.

For Warren, the break-up was a blow to the heart. He was devastated. "Susie," he told his sister, "was the sun and the rain in my garden for twenty-five years." But he slowly recovered as Susie led her own life, and together they kept some family traditions. They traveled together on many of Warren's frequent business trips. They also made their annual two-week excursion to New York and joined the kids at the Laguna Beach home for Christmas and other holidays.

6

CHERRY COKES AND BLACK MONDAY

At the end of each year, Berkshire Hathaway published an annual report that revealed the names of companies in which it had made major investments. By the end of 1979, these included not only GEICO but such household names as General Foods, F. W. Woolworth, and American Broadcasting, among many others. Berkshire's portfolio was so diverse because stock-market prices were down. The Dow had dropped into the 800's, lower than it had been in more than 10 years. The American economy was flat and likely to stay flat for some time. Inflation was zooming as high as 13 percent a year.

All that, to Warren Buffett, added up to a good time to buy stock in companies that met his criteria: those where stock prices were reasonable, the long-term future was promising, and management was both expert and trustworthy. In the Berkshire annual reports, Warren began writing essays that put forth his ideas simply and clearly. Readers of *Forbes* and other leading business magazines also began to see his words and ideas in print. If they checked on the price of shares in Berkshire, they found it was worth $290 per share in 1979, then $375 in 1980, despite the bear market in Wall Street. And Warren Buffett's personal fortune stood at $140 million or more. Most people who could figure out his net worth, however, were not aware that he limited his annual salary to $100,000 and had only recently raised it from $50,000.

April 1979 brought vindication to Warren in the dispute between the *Buffalo Evening News* and the *Courier-Express*. The U.S. Court of Appeals in New York ruled that the previous judge had been wrong. "Taking first the issue of intent," said the court's decision, "we find simply no evidence that Mr. Buffett acquired the News with the idea of putting the Courier out of business as distinguished from providing vigorous competition, including the invasion of what had been the Courier's exclusive Sunday market. All that the record supports is a finding that Mr. Buffett intended to do as well as he could with the News and was not lying awake thinking what the effect of its competition on the Courier would be. This is what the antitrust laws aim to promote, not to discourage."

Within two months after the court decision, the Cowles family of Minneapolis, owners of the Minneapolis Star & Tribune Company, bought the *Courier-Express*. The paper was still the best-seller on Sunday, while the *Evening News* was losing big money—$4.6 million in 1979 alone—trying to beat it.

In 1980 Warren turned 50. To honor the occasion, old friends and new, from high school chum Donald Danly to *Washington Post* publisher Kay Graham, gathered in New York for a formal party that Susie arranged. Warren entertained them with a balance sheet from the Wilson Coin Operated Machine Company. Susie, singing to him in her throaty cabaret style, brought tears to many eyes.

A Close Call and a Wider Audience

During the summer of 1981 Warren and a couple of friends met Charlie Munger for a few days' vacation at a cabin Charlie owned on a Minnesota lake. While they were fishing in Charlie's boat, Charlie put the outboard motor in reverse. Water flowed up over the transom at the stern. Charlie, whose eyesight was extremely poor, mistakenly increased the power. In seconds, the boat filled, flipped over, and trapped Warren beneath it. One of the men, a strong swimmer, pulled him out. All joked about the experience, nicknaming Charlie "Commodore Munger," but Warren had nearly drowned.

Warren was now earning a wider and wider audience. His essays in the Berkshire annual report were photocopied and distributed in banking circles and stockbroker offices in Wall Street and across America. Unlike the dry-as-dust annual reports of other corporations, the Berkshire reports were compared to the witty newspaper columns of a great American humorist, Will Rogers—and even to the long-respected commonsense writings of Benjamin Franklin in *Poor Richard's Almanac*. What readers liked best was Warren's uncanny ability to explain complicated financial subjects in ways that anybody could understand.

Readers noticed that Warren's essays most often addressed any of three main subjects. The first was inflation. He was scared of it and thought it was a problem that was never going away. He urged investors to buy shares in companies that produced well-known consumer brands, the prices of which could be raised to match inflation.

Another favorite subject was chief executive officers (CEOs), the heads of corporations. Warren wrote that too many CEOs let their egos take charge of their common sense as they managed. Most tried to build huge companies rather than respectable profits. Warren said that by buying up smaller companies and merging company into company, many CEOs built up their own domains while their shareholders—whom they were supposed to be serving—paid for the change.

The third subject was corporate management itself. Warren made it clear to his readers that the manager at the head of a company bears a heavy responsibility to the shareholders who provide the money that fuels the company. He wrote, for example, that it is wrong for a CEO to decide on where the company should do its charitable giving. The money being donated by the company, he pointed out, is actually the shareholders' money and they should have a say in where it goes.

In Buffalo, in the meantime, the Minneapolis owners of the *Courier-Express* decided to close the paper, which was losing $3 million a year despite still owning the Sunday readers. The day it closed, Warren took the word "evening" off his paper's masthead and began publishing a morning edition of the *Buffalo News*.

Buying 77 Acres of Furniture

In 1983 America's largest furniture store was the Nebraska Furniture Mart in Omaha. Its proprietor was Rose Blumkin, an 89-year-old who had started her business in 1937 in a storefront a block from the Buffett grocery store. Standing four feet and 10 inches tall, she had worked seven days a week, 52 weeks a year building her business on her motto, "Sell cheap and tell the truth." Rose was now selling $100 million worth of furniture every year, totaling two thirds of all Omaha furniture sales. Her store was so large it covered 77 acres. To move around fast so she could keep a sharp eye on sales clerks, Rose drove a golf cart in the aisles.

One morning that summer, Warren Buffett walked in. Rose knew him and Susie as good customers. He asked Rose if she would sell the Mart to Berkshire Hathaway. She said she would. He asked her price. She said, "Sixty million." He wrote her a check for 90 percent, keeping Rose and her three sons on the job as minority owners. As usual, Warren was making sure that those who knew the business best stayed on to run it.

Buying the Furniture Mart worked out so well that Warren soon talked with Rose's sister and her husband, who ran Borsheim's—a jewelry store in Omaha that used Rose's method of selling at low prices but profiting from high volume. Nationally, it was second only to Tiffany's in New York in total sales. Warren bought Borsheim's.

"A nine-hundred-pound gorilla"

Warren's phone rang in February 1985 with a call from Tom Murphy, chairman of Capital Cities, a company that Murphy had built up from a start in Albany, New York, by buying cable television systems and television and radio stations. For some years, Warren had advised Murphy as Capital Cities grew. Murphy said he was buying the ABC network (once known as the American Broadcasting Company). The buy, he said, would create a problem: Cap Cities (as it was called) would become so big that some other large corporation would want to try a takeover—that is, to assume control of the company by buying up the majority of its stock at whatever price it took to do so.

"You better have a nine-hundred-pound gorilla," said Warren. "Somebody who owns a significant amount of shares who will not sell regardless of price."

"How about you being the gorilla?" said Murphy.

Berkshire Hathaway agreed to buy 3 million shares of Cap Cities at $172.50 per share, or roughly half a billion dollars. It was eight times more than Warren had paid for Rose Blumkin's Furniture Mart and 50 times more than he had invested in *The Washington Post*. In effect, Berkshire's investment gave Cap Cities the force to buy ABC.

A few months later, Warren had Berkshire spend $315 million to buy a conglomerate—that is, a corporation that owns smaller corporations—named Scott Fetzer. Among its products were Kirby vacuum cleaners, Quikut knives, and *World Book Encyclopedia*. Before the year's end, Warren saw General Foods, in which Berkshire was the largest stockholder, taken over by the Philip Morris company, producing a $332 million profit for Berkshire. That made one share in Berkshire Hathaway worth $2,600 and put Warren Buffett on *Forbes* magazine's list of American billionaires. In Omaha alone, his Berkshire Hathaway had created 50 millionaires, and its stockholders around the country included hundreds more.

For years, Warren had poked fun at corporate jet airplanes, saying they were an unnecessary fringe benefit for executives. In 1986, however, he had Berkshire buy a used Falcon jet for $850,000. He admitted that as he traveled more and more his privacy was often invaded by fellow passengers who recognized him and tried to get him to talk about stock prices and recommend investments. He immediately fell in love with the jet, finding that it not only saved him time but gave him back his privacy, for its cabin was like a part of his office.

"I am a computer."

In early 1986, one share of Berkshire Hathaway was worth more than $3,000. That was 167 times higher than the $18 price when Warren took charge of the textile mill 21 years earlier. The Dow, in the same period, had only doubled. But Warren Buffett's lifestyle—and officestyle—remained simple. He answered his own phone. He kept no formal calendar to schedule his time. His desk had no calculator or stock ticker or computer.

Whether he is addressing stockholders or planning his personal schedule, Warren likes to keep things direct and simple.
(Associated Press)

When one visitor asked where his computer was, he replied, "I am a computer."

While they were growing up, the Buffett kids never knew they were well-to-do. They went to public schools and lived in a rather plain home on a busy street. Now that they were grown, they knew that their father loved them deeply but was not going to support them. If one of them wanted to borrow some money, Warren asked for— and got—a signed loan agreement clearly stating how it was to be repaid. On one occasion, young Susie needed $20 to pay for parking at the airport. Her father handed her the money and insisted she write him a check repaying him.

More and more, the Buffett children could read about their father in magazines and newspapers. In April 1985, for example, *New York* magazine headlined a feature, "Aw, Shucks, It's Warren Buffett." It described billionaire Buffett as a likable ordinary guy and, to prove that point, said he was "a chronic guzzler of Pepsi-Cola, preferably laced with cherry syrup." The president of Coca-Cola, Don Keough, read the story. In younger days, he had been an Omaha neighbor of Warren and had passed up the chance to buy a Buffett Partnership. Now he wrote to Warren, inviting him to try his company's new Cherry Coke, which was just being introduced. Warren switched colas and never looked back.

Cherry Cokes were everywhere—can upon can in giant tubs of ice—when Berkshire Hathaway shareholders gathered in Omaha for the company's annual meeting in 1986. The meeting was becoming a major event with nearly 500 participants, most of whom had their life savings tied up in Berkshire stock. The shareholders came to admire and be inspired by Warren, a plain-looking, glasses-wearing, tousle-haired man in rumpled gray slacks and blue blazer who was like a god to them. They came to hear his corny jokes and easy banter with his sidekick, Charlie Munger. To their delight, Warren and Charlie enlightened the throng hour after hour with their opinions on investments and inflation or their insight into Cap Cities/ABC or Rose Blumkin's management skills.

Over the next year, the companies in which Berkshire had majority ownership, and those it owned outright, produced more and more cash. Premiums from Berkshire's insurance companies, led by National Indemnity, rose to $1 billion in 1986, yielding $800 million of float. By 1987, the float was more than $1 billion. But finding low-priced stocks to buy with the money was a problem, for Wall Street was enjoying a thriving bull market. By August, the Dow had zoomed to 2,722.4 points and a single share of Berkshire Hathaway was at a record high: $4,270.

October 19: Black Monday

In his usual fashion, Warren disciplined himself against buying stocks during Wall Street's bull market. Instead, he bought municipal bonds in vast quantities. At the same time, in September he "sold high," as Wall Streeters would say, selling off Berkshire's extensive portfolio while he could get top prices. He kept only three stocks, which he called "permanent": the Washington Post company, GEICO, and Cap Cities.

Then, on Tuesday, October 6, 1987, the Dow set a one-day record by dropping 91.55 points. Ten days later it broke that record by falling 108 points. And on Monday, October 19, it lost 508 points, a drop of 22.6 percent in one day. Wall Street was in panic as every stockholder tried to sell off shares before prices dropped further.

Warren Buffett looked on calmly as Wall Streeters dubbed the day "Black Monday." He had already sold every stock he wanted to sell, each at its top price, while the bull market was at its peak. Even so, he had to face the fact that Black Monday had cut $342 million from his own net worth. And one share of Berkshire Hathaway had dropped from $4,230 a week earlier to $3,170 at the close of Black Monday.

7

A BILLION DOLLARS WORTH OF COKES

Warren went back to work, studying annual reports and balance sheets that showed what happened to companies after Black Monday. He saw that stock in the Coca-Cola Company had dropped 25 percent below its high point in the bull market. He read everything he could find on Coca-Cola, even 50-year-old articles in business magazines. Then he quietly put his Omaha stockbroker to work buying shares in Coca-Cola. They were the first common stocks he had bought in three years.

Coca-Cola executives noticed that a Nebraska stockbroker was buying large blocks of company stock. Their president, Don Keough, had a hunch. He phoned his old neighbor Warren and asked if he happened to be buying shares of Coca-Cola. "It so happens that I am," said Warren.

By March 1989, Berkshire Hathaway was Coca-Cola's largest shareholder, in effect owning nearly 7 percent of the company, a holding worth $1.02 billion. That month readers of *The Wall Street Journal* found out about Berkshire Hathaway's investment in the soft drink. Those smart enough—and lucky enough—to own Berkshire stock saw it rise over the next six months from $4,800 a share to more than $8,000, an increase of 66 percent.

Why did Warren want to buy Coca-Cola stock? He saw that in 1984 just about half of the company's profits came from sales overseas, but by 1987 that international trade had grown to three-quarters of the profits. From Brazil to Egypt, from Britain to the Philippines, in more and more countries, Coca-Cola was marketing its thirst-quencher. "What I then perceived," wrote Warren in his 1989 Berkshire Hathaway annual report, "was both clear and fascinating. What was already the world's most ubiquitous product had gained new momentum, with sales overseas virtually exploding."

That annual report also let Berkshire stockholders know that the *Buffalo News*, after several years of disconcerting losses, was now earning more than $40 million every year. It was reaching three out of every four Buffalo households—a better ratio than that of any other U.S. metropolitan newspaper.

Rose Blumkin Walks Out

The spring of 1989 brought an unusual event in Warren Buffett's business life. A headline in the _Omaha World-Herald_ summed it up: "Mrs. B: 'I Got Mad and Quit.'" In a dispute with her grandsons, who were now running the Furniture Mart but had left the management of the carpet department to her, the 95-year-old spitfire Rose Blumkin had walked out on them and, in effect, on Warren Buffett. Until then, no manager had ever quit on him.

To show he cared, Warren took Rose 24 pink roses for her birthday. But he showed his practical business side in the next Berkshire Hathaway annual report, saying, "Mrs. B probably has made more smart business decisions than any living American, but in this particular case I believe the other members of the family were entirely correct: Over the past three years, while the store's other departments increased sales by 24%, carpet sales declined."

Mrs. B thought about things for a few months. Then Warren and all Omaha became aware that a new carpet store, Mrs. B's Warehouse, had opened near the Furniture Mart.

Paper, Razors, and Charge Cards

The cash was still flowing in from the insurance companies, See's Candy Shops, the Furniture Mart, Scott Fetzer, the *Buffalo News*, and other Berkshire properties. Something had to be done with it. In the autumn of 1989, Warren looked at three companies that larger companies were eyeing as possible targets for takeovers. They were Champion International, producers of paper; Gillette, makers of razors and other personal products; and airline USAir. Knowing that each would welcome a "900-pound gorilla," Warren had Berkshire invest a total of $1.3 billion in them.

Critics noted that each company had created a new kind of stock, called a "convertible preferred" for the deal with Warren. A *Wall Street Journal* headline announced, "Heard on the Street: Buffett's Savior Role Lands Him Deals Other Holders Can't Get." But the fact was that the deal required Berkshire not only to hold the stocks for 10 years—a length of time no Wall Street firm ever committed to—but to live with dividends that were set in advance for that period. Warren himself was not crazy about the deal. "If I had four more Coca-Colas to buy," he said, "I wouldn't be buying these."

He bought something else that fall: a new $6.7 million jet airplane, jokingly christening it "The Indefensible." Now he was back and forth across the country or the

Atlantic, playing bridge in London with magazine publisher Malcolm Forbes, dining at the White House with President George H.W. Bush, or enjoying a pre-Academy-Awards dinner with country singer Dolly Parton. He turned up on television's *Lifestyles of the Rich and Famous* and even had the fun of playing a small role on TV's daytime soap opera *Loving*.

The situation changed again the next year. Early in 1990, one share of Berkshire was down from its September high of $8,750 to less than $8,000. Wall Street turned again to fear. By August, a real recession was in progress, with banks failing all across the country. At year's end, bankers knew they had seen their worst year since the Great Depression of the 1930's and Warren himself knew that Berkshire stock was back down to $5,500. Now he looked at one bank that had always intrigued him: San Francisco's Wells Fargo bank. Its stock was down from $84 a share to $58. He bought 10 percent of the bank's entire stock.

American Express was next. With the stock market rallying and the Dow climbing again in early 1991, Warren responded to a call from his friend James D. Robinson III, chairman of American Express. The charge-card company had wasted hard-earned profits on unwise investments. To help straighten it out, Warren agreed to meet Robinson's request for a $300 million investment from Berkshire. As

Charlie Munger and the Berkshire staff members knew, it was unlike Warren to make major investments when the market was high. But they also knew that he had a soft spot in his heart for American Express—dating from his profitable experience 25 years earlier—and, besides, with the market high again, there were few places where Berkshire's ever-increasing supply of cash income could be safely invested.

A Call at 7:00 A.M.

Among Warren Buffett's many investments was Salomon Brothers, a Wall Street investment bank that specialized in buying and re-selling U.S. Treasury bonds. By 1991, he held more Salomon stock than anybody—a total of $700 million worth. On Friday, August 16, his phone awakened him at 7:00 A.M. with a call from Salomon's managing partner, John Gutfreund. Salomon was in deep trouble.

Warren already knew, from phone calls over the past several weeks, that Salomon's partner who was in charge of buying government bonds had broken Treasury department rules by making bids—some as high as $1 billion—that his customers had not authorized. Now, said Gutfreund, the New York Federal Reserve Bank was about to cut off Salomon's right to deal in Treasury bonds—a market that was the world's largest, buying and selling

$100 billion worth of securities every day (the entire New York Stock Exchange bought and sold only $8 billion worth daily).

The cut-off would put Salomon Brothers out of business, hurting not only employees but the many investors who, like Warren, had bought stock in the firm. Gutfreund added that he and other top managing partners were about to resign, but they needed a man like Warren to take over. In effect, only he could save the firm.

This was the kind of mess that Warren had always carefully avoided. But he thought about the fact that as a business Salomon Brothers was strong and prospering. Now it was the victim of its own poor management, which had not kept a watchful eye on what some senior partners were doing. He flew to New York that day, spent the weekend in meetings with Salomon partners and Federal Reserve officials, and talked by phone with U.S. Secretary of the Treasury Nicholas Brady. The government officers agreed to let Salomon continue under Warren's direction as chairman.

Over the next several months, Warren worked to reorganize the thinking at Salomon Brothers, which had the habit of paying enormous bonuses to its partners, salesmen, and stock analysts while treating its shareholders like distant cousins. He endured weeks, then months, of unfavorable publicity in such publications as *The Wall*

Street Journal, Business Week, and *The New Republic*. He fought a demand from the U.S. Department of Justice and the Securities and Exchange Commission that Salomon pay $400 million in fines and plead guilty to a felony, finally reaching a settlement that cost Salomon $290 million and dismissed the felony charge.

In June 1992, after nine months as chairman, Warren chose Berkshire's lawyer as his successor and went back to Omaha. By then, under his direction, Salomon stock was worth 25 percent more than when the bad news broke the preceding August.

Rose Blumkin Returns

The year 1992 saw Warren Buffett back in Rose Blumkin's favor. At age 99, she settled her disputes with her grandsons, admitted to reporters that she had made a mistake, and sold Mrs. B's Warehouse to Berkshire Hathaway for $5 million. There she took charge of the carpet business, working seven days a week. "I am delighted that Mrs. B has again linked up with us," wrote Warren in his annual report. "Her business story has no parallel."

Neither, of course, did his own business story. Over the next couple of years, he paid $650 million for three manufacturers of shoes. He bought 14 percent of the stock in General Dynamics, a leading maker of military defense systems and jet aircraft for business, at $11 a share and saw it nearly quadruple, rising to $43.50. He bought sizeable blocks of stock in Gannett Newspapers and other companies. And he added to his investment in the Wells Fargo bank, paying $62 a share and then seeing his money more than double to $145 a share.

Shares of Berkshire Hathaway itself kept growing in value. At the end of 1992, the price per share was more than $10,000. A year later it was $16,325. In 1994, it reached $20,400. By then, anyone who had invested $10,000 in Berkshire in 1965 had become a millionaire more than 11 times over. The stock had grown at a compound rate of 26.77 percent a year, while the Dow saw 9.51 percent a year. And Warren Buffett's net worth stood at $9.7 billion.

8

THE ART OF PUTTING IN CASH

"We've really made the money out of high quality businesses," said Charlie Munger in a speech in 1994. "In some cases, we bought the whole business. And in some cases, we just bought a big block of stock. But when you analyze what happened, the big money's been made in the high quality businesses."

It did not always work. When Warren bought the three shoe manufacturers, only 30 percent of the shoes sold to Americans were made in America. Three years later, only 5 percent were American, Berkshire's income from shoe sales was 18 percent less, and its profit from the operation was 57 percent less. The numbers proved that Warren, who had expected U.S. customers to lose interest in imported shoes, could be wrong.

One thing he did not do was butt in. He stuck to his theory that those managers he kept in place when he bought a company should be allowed to do their jobs their own way. "With almost every one of the companies Berkshire owns," he said soon after the unsuccessful shoe experience, "I think I would do something different if I was running them—in some cases, substantially different." But, he added, he did not interfere because, "I sort of accept things as they come."

The Yellow BRK'ers and The Wizard of Omaha

Warren still liked his hamburgers. As if to prove that, in 1995, he had Berkshire buy 4.3 percent of the massive McDonald's Corporation. The total number of people employed by companies in which Berkshire was either the owner or a major shareholder now came to 23,783. In a sense, Warren Buffett could control whether or not they had jobs.

Both Warren and Susie Buffett were now traveling so often that a second jet plane was ordered as a personal plane for their use. Susie named it "The Richly Deserved." Seeing that, Warren renamed Berkshire's "The Indefensible," calling it "The Indispensable." Meantime, Berkshire Hathaway stock continued climbing as if it were itself a jet, reaching $30,000 per share in 1995.

By 1996, annual meetings of Berkshire Hathaway stockholders had grown into social events that were like college reunions. Old friends gathered from all across America and from even farther away. They came not only to hear the amusing and informative reports from Charlie Munger and Warren, who had become known as the "Wizard of Omaha." They eagerly boarded chartered buses to ride to shopping sprees at the Furniture Mart and at Borsheim's jewelry store.

That year, when one of them appeared in a big yellow hat, they added a special identification for Berkshire shareholders. Soon yellow hats were everywhere. Someone, with the Wizard in mind, named the hat-wearing group "The Yellow Brick Road." This was quickly shortened to "Yellow Brickers" and then "Yellow BRK'ers," which was soon printed on T-shirts.

The Yellow BRK'ers were pleased the same year when they learned that Berkshire had bought 49 percent of GEICO. Since it already owned 51 percent, it now had another fully owned property. The deal, which involved buying out GEICO stockholders for $70 per share in cash, increased Berkshire's total annual float to $7 billion.

Then there was FlightSafety International, a company that trained airline pilots. Berkshire bought it in 1996 for $1.5 billion. Warren kept its 79-year-old founder, Albert L. Ueltschi, on the job as CEO because, as Ueltschi said,

"I like what I do so much that I don't consider it work." That was Warren Buffett's kind of talk.

Warren's interest in aviation businesses was stretching into new areas. In July 1998, he had Berkshire spend $725 million to buy Executive Jet Aviation Inc. The company was a pioneer in providing corporate jet planes on a "time-share" basis. This gave businesses that did not need full-time jets, or could not afford them, a chance to have them when they did need them. "It's clearly a field," said Warren, "that is going to explode over the next decade."

Warren appears at a news conference with banking and insurance commissioner Holly Bakke and Gecko, the GEICO insurance company's mascot. (Associated Press)

August brought sad news. At the age of 104, Rose Blumkin died. Only two days earlier, she had been at work in the Nebraska Furniture Mart. "They'll be studying her in business history books for decades," said Warren. "It was brains, intelligence, her wouldn't-be-stopped drive."

Six Hours of Q and A

By May 1998, it took Omaha's convention center, Aksarben Stadium, to hold the crowd of 11,000 attending Berkshire Hathaway's annual meeting. There amid the tubs of Cherry Cokes and countless tables covered with ample trays of See's Candies, the throng was enthralled as Warren, along with Charlie Munger, covered annual-meeting business in only five minutes. They then settled into nearly six hours of questions and answers. One reporter from a business magazine came away with page after page of notes on what Warren and Charlie said. A few of them follow:

- Time is the enemy of poor businesses, the friend of good businesses.
- Our central role is to motivate the chairmen of our companies to keep working even though they are already very rich.
- Buy stocks that you never want to sell; when you get a good business, buy for life.

- Coca-Cola is the best large business in the world.
- Look for candid, clear, coherent prose. If a business has a problem, we would like to know about it. Honesty and openness is the best policy.
- Investing is the art of putting in cash now to get more cash later on.
- We like homey, Norman Rockwell types of companies.
- Learn all the accounting you can.
- My principle is to leave enough money for your children that they can do anything they want, but not enough so that they can do nothing.

Onstage: Daddy Warrenbucks

By December 1998, *Fortune* magazine's list of America's 500 largest companies showed Berkshire Hathaway as 112th in total income and 32nd in profits. Now Warren Buffett steered his company into its biggest buy yet, spending $22 billion to acquire the General Re Corporation. It is what is known in the insurance business as a reinsurance company. In effect, it provided insurance policies that protected smaller insurance companies against failure if they suddenly had to pay larger numbers of claims than they had anticipated. (For example, such an event might occur in the aftermath of a major hurricane, a time when casualty claims can reach huge numbers.)

With General Re added, Berkshire Hathaway's annual float now climbed to $22 billion while the company's total number of shareholders came to about 250,000. Their shareholder equity—that is, the amount of money their stock would turn into if they all sold it at the same time—was worth $57 billion. This was second only to the highest, the Royal Dutch/Shell Group, among all companies in the world, and was far higher than Microsoft, General Electric, or any other U.S. corporation. And, counting all the companies Berkshire owned and operated, some 45,000 employees could say that they worked for Warren Buffett. Of those, only 12 worked in the company headquarters in Omaha.

The numbers kept growing. By the Berkshire 1999 annual meeting in May, its employees numbered 47,566 (double the number in 1995) and the company owned $124 billion in assets. Warren himself now held $15 billion in cash and—at least on paper—could count up another $30 billion in gains made, but not turned into cash, in stocks held in Berkshire's portfolios.

Of Berkshire Hathaway's 280,000 shareholders in 1999, 15,000 showed up for the annual meeting, overflowing the Aksarben Coliseum. Those who wanted the best seats were in line as early as 4:15 A.M. to wait for the doors to open officially at 7:00. Warren arrived at 6:30 A.M. to greet the lineup of dedicated shareholders. Late arrivals had to accept places in nearby rooms where they could watch the meeting on closed-circuit TV.

Aside from official business, the daylong event included—among other goodies and souvenirs—bushel after bushel of individually wrapped chocolates from See's Candies, big red Coca-Cola shopping bags, GEICO flashlight keychains, and Disney "I love Berkshire Hathaway" buttons featuring Mickey Mouse. A specially-produced movie kept the crowd laughing for an hour with profiles of Warren and Charlie that featured Warren—always the amateur songbird—singing in his unique but on-key style. It included videotape of Warren playing the role of Daddy Warbucks (renamed "Warrenbucks" for the occasion) in a local charity production of the stage musical *Annie*, as well as scenes from his appearance, along with his friend Tom Murphy, on the television soap opera *All My Children*.

One highlight of the day came when the crowd watched Warren throw out the first pitch at a minor-league baseball game featuring the Omaha Golden Spikes—a team to which Warren had paid $1.25 million to become a 25-percent owner. Hundreds of Yellow BRK'ers were present in their oversized hats, crowding around Warren as he patiently signed his autograph on hats, scraps of paper, and even a $20 bill. As an hour or more went by, they noticed that several bodyguards constantly stayed close to him.

As exhausting as Warren's schedule was when he made such public appearances, he seemed to thrive on it. "Except for my voice," he told London reporters in the spring of 1999 during a busy tour of England, Germany, and France to promote Berkshire's Executive Jet Aviation, "I never get tired." Those who traveled with him endured four-course banquets, two-hour lunches, and unending press conferences. If they lost track of his whereabouts, they knew that if they followed the next waiter they saw delivering Coca-Cola they would be led to him.

9

A LIFE FILLED WITH BIG NUMBERS

By August 1999, anyone who wanted to buy one share of Berkshire Hathaway had to pay $68,000 for it. Warren Buffett himself owned 38 percent of the company, giving him a net worth of $36 billion. At the age of 68, he was the second wealthiest person in the world. Only Microsoft's Bill Gates had more. Yet home was still the stucco house that Susie and Warren bought for $31,500 in 1956, and lunch or dinner was most often hamburgers and Coca-Cola.

That fall Warren took another daring step. Studying the utilities business (mostly gas pipelines and electric power) he saw that investors were pouring money into unregulated companies but not into those that were regulated. (Regulated utilities charge rates that are regulated by government and have customers who are guaranteed to be theirs; unregulated utilities produce power on speculation, predicting how much they think they can sell, and charge whatever their customers are willing to pay.) Once again, Warren saw value. Stockbrokers and their investors were ignoring regulated companies. He seized an opportunity for Berkshire to buy, at a cost of $3.3 billion, 80 percent of MidAmerican Energy Holdings Co., which owned regulated utilities in Iowa, California, and Great Britain. He did not know that within two years unregulated utilities, led by the dramatic breakdown of a Texas company called Enron, would be collapsing, leaving shareholders

Two of the world's wealthiest men: Warren Buffett and Microsoft chairman, Bill Gates (WireImage)

empty handed and wishing they had bought stock in regulated companies.

As the millennium year 2000 rolled around, Warren saw that the bubble of high-technology stocks that had been stretching higher and wider for 10 years was beginning to burst. He had never bought any of the thousands of get-rich-quick shares that had been offered—not even such industry leaders as Hewlett-Packard and Microsoft. If asked why he did not invest in high-tech, his answer had been simple: No one could predict how much such companies would earn over 10 or 20 years. "I can't do it myself," he said. "And if I don't know, I don't invest."

The Man on the Cover

By 2002, the editors of *Fortune* magazine, which had been following the fortunes of Warren Buffett for nearly 40 years, decided to produce a cover story on him. They went to work with business journalist Andy Serwer to create the 10-page feature, which appeared in the November 11 issue. "What may surprise Buffett fans," said a note on the Editor's Desk page, "is how much the man rocks, not only because he's making good bets in the market these days but also because he's buying—and managing—good companies. 'Berkshire Hathaway may be the most singular FORTUNE 500 business ever,' says Andy Serwer. 'It shouldn't work, but it does.' To bring you Buffett's latest thinking (and doings),

Serwer hung out with the man for a frantic 48 hours, traveling from his home base in Omaha to a heavy-hitting golf outing at fabled Pebble Beach, Calif."

Among the many facts revealed by the *Fortune* story was that Warren now employed 145,296 people in companies ranging from Shaw Industries (the world's largest maker of tufted broadloom carpet) with 28,200 workers to Precision Steel with 200. The graph showing them listed 35 different companies. But more important than such numbers was the way Serwer summed up what he saw in Warren Buffett. "He not only has been dead-on with the vast majority of his investments over time," he wrote, "but has also—in his own calm, self-effacing, almost goofy way—been right about much else: right on his views about corporate governance, right about stock options and accounting reform, right about the demise of corporate ethics, uncannily right about the stock market."

The *Fortune* story, like Warren Buffett's life by 2002, was filled with big numbers. It revealed, for example, that Warren would no longer consider buying any company that showed less than $50 million in annual profits before taxes, and that the cash coming into Berkshire Hathaway each year from its operating companies, investments, and insurance float totaled $5 billion. "We've got $100 million a week that I have to figure out what to do with," Warren told journalist Serwer. "It's a happy problem, but it's a problem, especially if I do something dumb with it—and that's easy to do."

Warren Speaks Out

The 14,000 people who went to Omaha for the 2003 annual meeting of Berkshire shareholders discovered a new side of Warren Buffett. He spoke out strongly against tax cuts proposed by President George W. Bush. "I am not for the Bush plan," he said. "It screams of injustice. The main beneficiaries will be people like me and Charlie." He added that the tax plan was like "us giving a lesser percentage of our incomes to Washington than the people working in our shoe factories."

He went on to say that investors should revolt against the huge salaries and bonuses paid to corporate executives. Over some 20 years there had been, he said, "an enormous disparity in the rates of compensation between people at the top and people at the bottom, and a disconnect between people at the top and the shareowners who give them the money."

Swooping his arms upward, he concluded, "Arise, shareholders."

In Arnold's Corner

Warren surprised his followers in August when Californians voted to recall their governor from office and actor Arnold Schwarzenegger ran as the Republican candidate to replace him. Warren, a registered Democrat known for backing that party's causes, said yes to an invitation from Schwarzenegger to serve as his senior financial and economic adviser.

Warren said he accepted because of the miserable condition of California's economy as well as the state's value

Warren, a registered Democrat, was a strong supporter of Republican Arnold Schwarzenegger's run for governor of California (Associated Press)

to the nation. He pointed out that property taxes in the state were too low, noting that he was paying only $2,264 in taxes on his $4 million home in Laguna Beach but he was paying a $14,401 tax on his Omaha home, which was currently evaluated at $500,000 (that is, the same house he bought in 1956 for $31,500).

As the year ended, Berkshire Hathaway counted up $19.86 billion in total income for 2003. That was a 64 percent increase over the $12.1 billion earned in 2002. Any investor who wanted to buy stock in Berkshire now had to pay $93,000 for a single share.

The growth continued. By New Year's 2004, Berkshire held shares in PetroChina, an oil and natural-gas company operating 29 refineries in China, that were worth more than $1.3 billion—almost three times what they cost Berkshire a few months earlier. Warren's buying stock in a utility in China showed how hard it now was for him to find stocks in the United States that, fitting his long-time basic criterion, were undervalued. Emphasizing that fact, he said, "We strongly prefer owning businesses to owning stocks."

As if to prove that distinction, early in 2004 Warren had Berkshire buy a bankrupt manufacturer of mobile homes, Oakwood Homes, for $373 million and announced his plan to make it the largest builder of such homes.

"Like a Religious Experience"

May brought a crowd of 20,000—the largest yet—to the Berkshire Hathaway annual meeting. Business reporters called it an investing seminar, a country fair, a carnival, and a revival meeting. The festivities began on Friday evening with a jam-packed buffet dinner on the huge sales floor of Borsheim's jewelry store. There the visitors could buy not only expensive baubles at big discounts but such Berkshire-marked souvenirs as golf balls, decks of cards, and matching Warren and Charlie dolls.

The Saturday meeting again opened with an hour-long film that featured Warren strumming his ukulele as he touchingly sang one of his old favorites, "Ain't She Sweet?" It also showed his wisecracking side as he exchanged quips with Bill Gates, Arnold Schwarzenegger, Jimmy Buffett, and Donald Trump. Then came the all-day Q and A session that everyone had been looking forward to for a year, with Warren and Charlie center stage. "It's a party," said one shareholder's wife. "Warren and Charlie are like a comedy team. They teach and they have fun."

"It's like a religious experience," said a mortgage broker from Chicago. "Everyone here, from Buffett and Munger on down, has the right attitude and values: honesty, integrity, decency. People here are the way you'd like everybody to be in life."

During the Q and A, one shareholder asked Warren what his worst mistake had been in recent years. "Wal-Mart," said Buffett. "We bought a little and it moved up a little and I thought maybe it will come back a bit. That thumbsucking has cost us in the current area of $10 billion."

Another asked whether Warren and Charlie worried about such major events as the war in Iraq. "We really don't pay any attention to that sort of thing," said Warren. "Our underlying premise is that this country will do very well, and it will do very well for businesses. American business really has never let investors down, but investors have done themselves in quite frequently."

The summer of 2004 brought dismaying news to the Buffetts' countless friends. At age 72 and with Warren at her side, Susie died of a stroke on July 29 while visiting in Cody, Wyoming. Earlier in the year, in *Forbes* magazine's annual listing of the richest Americans, she had been 60th, while her husband was listed again as second only to Bill Gates. Susie's net worth at the time of her death was $3.1 billion and she owned 2 percent of Berkshire Hathaway. One share of Berkshire was then priced at more than $87,000.

10

"I GET TO DO WHAT I LIKE"

At the time of the 2004 annual meeting of Berkshire Hathaway, 73-year-old Warren Buffett still owned 38 percent of that company. His net worth was now estimated to be $42.9 billion. His wealth was still second only to that of Microsoft's Bill Gates.

By this time, people were beginning to ask who might succeed Warren as head of Berkshire Hathaway. Could anyone, they asked, run the business as astutely as he did? In an interview in 1999, Warren had said he had two people in mind to take charge—one to run the operating companies that Berkshire owns outright, and the other to manage its vast portfolio of investments—but he would not say who they were.

Asked about that, Charlie Munger said, "The one place a death will hurt us is we're not likely to get as good an allocator of capital as Warren in the next CEO, whoever that is. The corporate culture of Berkshire is more durable than that of the average corporation. That will go on."

As to where his money will go, Warren has said that he intends to leave 99 percent of his estate to the Buffett Foundation, which he established in 1964. When (or if) that happens, it will become the world's best-endowed foundation, larger than the long-standing Ford or Rockefeller foundations or the $27 billion Bill & Melinda Gates Foundation, which was established in 1994. The Buffett Foundation has given money over many years— usually from $10 million to $15 million a year—to Planned Parenthood, education, and efforts to reduce the risk of nuclear war. Warren has not said what he would want it to support after his lifetime.

A Chocolate Sundae and Roller Skates

As he turned 75 in 2005, Warren continued to drive his own car—no limos for him—and maintain his simple down-to-earth attitude. If he felt like eating peanuts and drinking Cherry Coke for breakfast, that was what he had. His Cap Cities friend Tom Murphy, in fact, can recall Warren's ordering a chocolate sundae for breakfast during a Super Bowl weekend.

When Andy Serwer interviewed Warren's secretary for his _Fortune_ cover story in 2002, she said, "I need roller skates to keep up with him, but I've never seen him get mad. I don't think he'd like to be lied to, though. If you make a mistake and tell him about it, that's okay, but you wouldn't want to cover it up."

That has been Warren Buffett's strength: the go-get-'em energy he was born with, the patience to see things through, and the direct honesty that was bred in his bones. That combination, steered by his strong self-discipline and common sense, made him a financial genius.

Has Warren Buffett offered any advice for young teenagers? Yes. Among the 20,000 people at the 2004 annual meeting of Berkshire Hathaway was a 14-year-old from California. During the Q and A for shareholders, he asked Warren and Charlie what advice they had for a young person on how to be successful. "It's better to hang out with people better than you," said Warren. "Pick out associates whose behavior is better than yours and you'll drift in that direction."

Charlie Munger added a comment, telling the teen not to worry "if this gives you a little temporary unpopularity with your peer group."

Warren sums up his situation in a few simple words. "I get to do what I like to do every single day of the year," he says. "I get to do it with people I like, and I don't have to associate with anybody who causes my stomach to churn. I tap dance to work, and when I get there I think I'm supposed to lie on my back and paint the ceiling. It's tremendous fun."

Readers of Berkshire's 2003 annual report caught Warren's usual spirit in his letter to shareholders, which he still wrote in his chummy style. Commenting on the immense tax bill for 2003—amounting to $3.3 billion—that his company was paying to the Internal Revenue Service, he wrote: "Our federal tax return for 2002, when we paid $1.75 billion, covered a mere 8,905 pages. As is required, we dutifully filed two copies of this return, creating a pile of paper seven feet tall. Berkshire, we felt, was surely pulling its share of our country's fiscal load."

Following that thought, Warren wrote: "If only 540 taxpayers paid the amount Berkshire will pay, no other individual or corporation would have to pay *anything* to Uncle Sam. That's right: 290 million Americans and all other businesses would not have to pay a dime in income, Social Security, excise or estate taxes to the federal government. (Here is the math: Federal tax receipts, including Social Security receipts, in fiscal 2003 totaled $1.782 trillion and 540 "Berkshires" each paying $3.3 billion, would deliver the same $1.782 trillion.)"

Writing these words seemed to stir Warren's memory. He composed a final paragraph for this section of his letter. "In 1944," he wrote, "I filed my first 1040 [tax return], reporting my income as a thirteen-year-old newspaper

About his career, Warren says with pride, "I get to do what I like every day of the year." (Corbis)

carrier. The return covered three pages. After I claimed the appropriate business deductions, such as $35 for a bicycle, my tax bill was $7. I sent my check to the Treasury and it—without comment—promptly cashed it. We lived in peace."

TIME LINE

1930 Born on August 30 in Omaha, Nebraska

1936 Buys Coca-Cola six-packs for 25 cents, resells bottles for 5 cents each

1939 Collects and sells used golf balls

1941 Buys three shares of Cities Service Preferred oil company at $38 per share and resells them at $40 per share

1943 Moves to Washington, D.C.; runs away to Hershey, Pennsylvania

1945 Makes $175 a month delivering Washington, D.C. newspapers; buys farm in Nebraska for $1,200

1946 Starts business placing pinball machines in barbershops; graduates from high school at 16; enters

University of Pennsylvania's Wharton School of Finance and Commerce

1949   Transfers to University of Nebraska at Lincoln; manages 50 newspaper delivery boys

1950   Application to Harvard University Graduate School of Business Administration is rejected; enters Columbia University Graduate School of Business and begins studies with mentor, Professor Ben Graham; discovers GEICO insurance company

1951   Graduates from Columbia with an A+; joins father's Omaha stock brokerage firm

1952   On April 19, marries Susan Thompson

1954   Joins Ben Graham's mutual fund staff in New York City

1956   Returns to Omaha; on May 1, launches Buffett Associates, Ltd.; buys five-bedroom home for $31,500

1962   Buffett Associates worth $7.2 million, Warren himself worth $1 million; merges firm into Buffett Partnerships, Ltd.; starts buying stock in Berkshire Hathaway textile company; Charlie Munger joins partnership

1965   Gains control of Berkshire Hathaway; uses its capital to buy National Indemnity insurance company

1966   Berkshire Hathaway assets total $44 million

1969   Liquidates all Buffett Partnership stocks except two: Berkshire Hathaway and Diversified Retailing; becomes Berkshire's largest shareholder

1971   Buys vacation home in Laguna Beach, California; buys See's Candy Shops

1973   Buys stock in *The Washington Post* and *Boston Globe*; becomes adviser to *Post* publisher Katharine Graham

1976   Invests $23 million in GEICO

1977   Buys *Buffalo Evening News*; Susie, now a cabaret singer, moves to an apartment in San Francisco

1981   Nearly drowns in boating accident

1983   Buys Rose Blumkin's Nebraska Furniture Mart

1985   Invests $500 million in Capital Cities; named on *Forbes* magazine list of American billionaires

1986   Buys jet airplane

1987   Sells off all stocks except three during bull market just before "Black Monday"

1989   Becomes Coca-Cola's largest shareholder

1991   Rescues Salomon Brothers investment bank from disaster following scandal

1998   Buys General Re reinsurance company for $22 billion

1999   Berkshire annual meeting has 15,000 attendees; throws out first ball at Omaha Golden Spikes minor-league baseball game; buys 80 percent of MidAmerican Energy Holdings Co. for $3.3 billion

2002   Featured in *Fortune* magazine cover story

2003   Speaks out against tax cuts for the wealthy; accepts invitation to serve as senior financial and economic adviser to Arnold Schwarzenegger, candidate for governor of California

2004   Owns 38 percent of Berkshire Hathaway; personal net worth at $42.9 billion

HOW TO BECOME A FINANCIAL SERVICES BROKER

THE JOB

Financial services brokers, sometimes called registered representatives, account executives, securities sales representatives, or stockbrokers, work to represent both individuals and organizations who wish to invest in and sell stocks, bonds, or other financial products. Financial services brokers analyze companies offering stocks to see if investing is worth the risk. They also advise clients on proper investment strategies for their own investment goals. Securities, commodities, and financial services brokers hold approximately 300,000 jobs in the United States.

The most important part of a broker's job is finding customers and building a client base. Beginning brokers spend much of their time searching for customers, relying heavily on telephone solicitation such as "cold calls"—calling people with whom they have never had any contact. Brokers also find customers through business and social contacts or they might be given a list of likely prospects from their brokerage firm.

When financial services brokers open accounts for new customers, they first record all the personal information that is required to allow the customer to trade securities through the brokerage firm. Depending on a customer's knowledge of the market, the broker may explain the meaning of stock market terms and trading practices and offer financial counseling. Then the broker helps the customer to devise an individual financial portfolio, including securities, life insurance, corporate and municipal bonds, mutual funds, certificates of deposit, annuities, and other investments. The broker must determine the customer's investment goals—such as whether the customer wants long-term, steady growth or a quick turnaround of stocks for short-term gains—and then offers advice on investments accordingly. Once an investment strategy has been developed, brokers execute buy and sell orders for their customers by relaying the information to the floor of the stock exchange, where the order is put into effect by the broker's floor representative. Securities traders also buy and sell securities, but usually as a representative of a private firm.

From the research department of the brokerage firm, brokers obtain information on the activities and projected growth of any company that is currently offering stock or plans to offer stock in the near future. The actual or perceived strength of a company is a major factor in a stock-purchase decision. Brokers must be prepared to answer questions on the technical aspects of stock market operations and also be informed on current economic conditions. They are expected to have the market knowledge to anticipate certain trends and to counsel customers accordingly in terms of their particular stock holdings.

Some financial services brokers specialize in areas such as institutional accounts, bond issues, or mutual funds. Whatever their area of specialization, financial services brokers must keep abreast of all significant political and economic conditions that might effect financial markets, maintain very accurate records for all transactions, and continually solicit new customers.

REQUIREMENTS

High School

If you are interested in becoming a financial services broker, you should take courses in business, accounting, economics, mathematics, government, and communications.

Postsecondary Training

Because of the specialized knowledge necessary to perform this job properly, a college education is increasingly important, especially in the larger brokerage houses. To make intelligent and insightful judgments, a broker must be able to read and understand financial reports and evaluate statistics. For this reason, although employers seldom require specialized academic training, a bachelor's degree in business administration, economics, or finance is helpful.

Certification or Licensing

Almost all states require brokers to be licensed. Some states administer written examinations and some require brokers to post a personal bond. Brokers must register as representatives of their firms with the National Association of Securities Dealers (NASD). In order to register with NASD, brokers must first pass the General Securities Registered Representative Examination (Series 7 exam) administered by NASD Regulation (a subsidiary of NASD) to demonstrate competence in the areas in which they will work. In addition, they must be employees of a registered firm for at least four months. Many states also require brokers to take and pass a second examination—the Uniform Securities Agents State Law Examination.

Other Requirements

Because they deal with the public, brokers should be well groomed and pleasant and have large reserves of tact and patience. Employers look for ambitious individuals with sales ability. Brokers also need self-confidence and the ability to handle frequent rejections. Above all, they must have a highly developed sense of responsibility, because in many instances they will be handling funds that represent a client's life savings.

EXPLORING

Any sales experience can provide you with a general background for work in financial services. You might be able to find summer employment in a brokerage house. A visit to a local investment office, the New York Stock Exchange, or one of the commodities exchanges located in other major cities will provide a valuable opportunity to observe how transactions are handled and what is required of people in the field.

EMPLOYERS

Financial services brokers and related workers hold about 300,000 jobs. The Department of Labor reports that seven out of 10 brokers work for securities and commodities firms, exchanges, and investment services companies. One in seven are employed by banks, savings institutions, and credit unions.

Financial services brokers work all around the country. Although many employers are very small, the largest employers of financial services brokers are a few large firms that have their main offices in major cities, especially New York.

STARTING OUT

Many firms hire beginning sales workers and train and retain them for a probationary period to determine their talents and ability to succeed in the business. The training period lasts about six months and includes classroom instruction and on-the-job training. Applications for these beginning jobs may be made directly to the personnel offices of the various securities firms. Check your local Yellow Pages or the Internet for listings of securities firms.

ADVANCEMENT

Depending upon their skills and ambitions, financial services brokers may advance rapidly in this field. Accomplished brokers may find that the size and number of accounts they service will increase to a point at which they no longer need to solicit new customers. Others become branch managers, research analysts, or partners in their own firms.

EARNINGS

The salaries of trainees and beginners range from $1,200 to $1,500 per month, although larger firms pay a somewhat higher starting wage. Once the financial services broker has acquired a sufficient number of accounts, he or she works solely on a commission basis, with fees resulting from the size and type of security bought or sold. Some firms pay annual bonuses to their brokers when business warrants. Since earnings can fluctuate greatly based on the condition of the market, some brokers may find it necessary to supplement their income through other means during times of slow market activity.

According to the U.S. Department of Labor, the median earnings for brokers were $60,990 a year in 2002; the middle 50 percent earned between $36,180 and $117,050. Ten percent earned less than $26,540, and 10 percent earned more than $145,000.

WORK ENVIRONMENT

Brokers work more flexible hours than workers in other fields. They may work fewer hours during slow trading periods but be required to put in overtime dealing with paperwork during busy periods.

The atmosphere of a brokerage firm is frequently highly charged, and the peaks and drops of market activity can produce a great deal of tension. Watching fortunes being made is exciting, but the reverse occurs frequently, too, and it requires responsibility and maturity to weather the setbacks.

OUTLOOK

The U.S. Department of Labor predicts that job opportunities for financial services brokers are expected to grow faster than the average for all occupations through 2012 because of continued interest in the stock market. Rising personal incomes and greater inherited wealth are increasing the amount of funds people are able to invest. Many people dabble in investing via their personal computers and the Internet. Even those with limited means have the option of investing through a variety of methods such as investment clubs, mutual funds, and monthly payment plans. In addition, the expansion of business activities and new technological breakthroughs will create increased demand for the sale of stock to meet capital requirements for companies around the world.

Demand for financial services brokers fluctuates with the economy. Turnover among beginners is high because they have a hard time soliciting enough clients. Because of potentially high earnings, competition in this business is very intense.

TO LEARN MORE ABOUT FINANCIAL SERVICES BROKERS

BOOKS

Darvas, Nicolas. *How I Made $2,000,000 in the Stock Market.* New York: Carol Publishing Group, 1986.

Karlitz, Gail, and Debbie Honig. *Growing Money: A Complete Investing Guide for Kids.* New York: Price Stern Sloan, 2001.

Morris, Kenneth M., and Virginia B. Morris. *The Wall Street Journal Guide to Understanding Money & Investing.* 3rd ed. Lightbulb Press, 2004.

Otfinoski, Steven. *The Kid's Guide to Money: Earning It, Saving It, Spending It, Growing It, Sharing It.* New York: Scholastic, 1996.

Smith, Pat, and Lynn Roney. *Wow the Dow! The Complete Guide to Teaching Your Kids How to Invest in the Stock Market.* New York: Simon and Schuster, 2000.

WEBSITES

To learn more about different types of investment professionals and new financial products and to read a glossary of terms and news alerts, visit the Individual Investor section of the National Association of Securities Dealers (NASD) website. Also visit the website for more information on NASD and its subsidiaries.

NASD/NASD Regulation

One Liberty Plaza, 48th Floor

New York, NY 10006

Tel: 301-590-6500

http://www.nasd.com

To learn more about investing, the securities industry, and industry issues, contact

The Securities Industry Association

120 Broadway, 35th Floor

New York, NY 10271-0080

Tel: 212-608-1500

Email: info@sia.com

http://www.sia.com

TO LEARN MORE ABOUT WARREN BUFFETT

BOOKS AND ARTICLES

Buffett, Warren. "Dividend Voodoo." *The Washington Post*, May 20, 2003.

Hagstrom, Robert G. *The Warren Buffett Way: Investment Strategies of the World's Greatest Investor*. New York: Wiley, 1995.

Kilpatrick, Andrew. *Of Permanent Value: The Story of Warren Buffett.* Birmingham, Alabama: Andy Kilpatrick Publishing Empire (AKPE), 2002.

Lavietes Stuart. "Philip A. Fisher, 96, Is Dead; Wrote Key Investment Book." *The New York Times*, April 19, 2004.

Lim, Paul J. "Investors: Do Not Try This at Home." *The New York Times*, March 14, 2004.

Lowe, Janet. *Warren Buffett Speaks: Wit and Wisdom from the World's Greatest Investor*. New York: Wiley, 1997.

Lowenstein, Roger. *Buffett: The Making of an American Capitalist*. New York: Random House, 1995.

Price, John. "The Return of the Buffetteers." *Investor Journal*, August 1998.

Serwer, Andy. "The Oracle of Everything." *Fortune*, November 11, 2002.

Train, John. *The Midas Touch: The Strategies That Have Made Warren Buffett "America's Pre-eminent Investor."* New York: Harper & Row, 1987.

Treaster, Joseph B. "Berkshire Hathaway Millionaires Gather." *The New York Times*, May 2, 2004.

"Berkshire Says 4th Quarter Profit Doubled." *The New York Times*, March 7, 2004.

"Berkshire Hathaway's Bid for Oakwood Is Approved." *The New York Times*, January 24, 2004.

WEBSITES

"Buffett slams dividend tax cut." CNN/Money website, May 20, 2003. Available online. URL: http://money.cnn.com/2003/05/20/news/buffett_tax/. Downloaded May 21, 2004.

"Is Warren Buffett Right?" rediff.com website, Associated Press (AP), March 18, 2004. Available online. URL: http://inhome.rediff.com/cms/print.jsp?docpath = /money/2004/mar/18guest.htm. Downloaded May 21, 2004.

"Warren Buffett." Wikipedia website. Available online. URL: http://en.wikipedia.org/w/wiki.phtml?title = Warren_Buffett&printable = yes. Downloaded May 21, 2004.

"Warren Buffett and the Incredible Rose Blumkin." Warren Buffett Secrets website. Available online. URL: http://www.buffettsecrets.com/rose-blumkin-nebraska-furniture-mart.htm. Downloaded May 21, 2004.

"Warren Buffett: How He Does It." Investopedia website. Available online. URL: http://www.investopedia.com/printable.asp?a = /articles/01/071801.asp. Downloaded May 20, 2004.

Bianco, Anthony. "The Warren Buffett You Don't Know." BusinessWeek Online website. Available online. URL: http://www.businessweek.com:/1999/99_27/b3636001.htm?scriptFramed. Downloaded May 20, 2004.

Buckingham, Marcus and Donald O. Clifton. "Warren Buffett and You." Gallup Management Journal website, January 29, 2001. Available online. URL: http://gmj.gallup.com/print/?ci = 550. Downloaded May 21, 2004.

Chang, Yi-Hsin. "Getting to Know Warren." The Motley Fool website. April 29, 1999. Available online. URL: http://www.fool.com/Server/FoolPrint.asp?File = / specials/1999/sp990429berkshire002.htm. Downloaded May 21, 2004.

———. "Pilgrimage to Omaha," Part 1. The Motley Fool website. May 2, 1999. Available online. URL: http:// www.fool.com/Server/FoolPrint.asp?File = /specials/ 1999/sp990502omaha002.htm. Downloaded May 21, 2004.

———. "Pilgrimage to Omaha," Part 2. The Motley Fool website. May 2, 1999. Available online. URL: http://www. fool.com/Server/FoolPrint.asp?File = /specials/1999/ sp990502omaha003.htm. Downloaded May 21, 2004.

———. "Pilgrimage to Omaha," Part 3. The Motley Fool website. May 4, 1999. Available online. URL: http://www. fool.com/Server/FoolPrint.asp?File = /specials/1999/ sp990502omaha004.htm. Downloaded May 21, 2004.

———."The Buffett & Munger Show." The Motley Fool website. May 6, 1999. Available online. URL: http://www. fool.com/Server/FoolPrint.asp?File = /specials/1999/ sp990502omaha005.htm. Downloaded May 21, 2004.

Kanter, Larry. "Warren Buffett." Salon website. August 31, 1999. Available online. URL: http://www.salon.com/ people/bc/1999/08/31/buffett/print.html. Downloaded April 17, 2004.

Kennon, Joshua. "Warren Buffett Biography: The Story of Berkshire Hathaway's Billionaire Chairman." About website. Available online. URL: http://beginnersinvest.about. com/cs/warrenbuffett/a/aawarrenbio_p.htm. Downloaded May 20, 2004.

Louderback, Jeff. "The Real Warren Buffett." NewsMax website, August 19, 2003. Available online. URL: http://www. newsmax.com/printer.cfm?page = http:/www.newsmax. com/archives/articles/2003/8/18/155747.shtml. Downloaded May 21, 2004.

Mann, Bill. "Warren Buffett and His 20 Punches." The Motley Fool website, May 5, 2004. Available online. URL: http://www.foolcom/Server/FoolPrint.asp?File = / news/commentary/2004/commentary040505bm.htm. Downloaded May 21, 2004.

Rayner, Abigail. "US sage attacks executive greed." Times Online website, May 5, 2003. Available online. URL: http:/www.timesonline.co.uk/printFriendly/0,,1-5-669779-5,00.html. Downloaded May 21, 2004.

Zweig, Jason. "Warren Buffett, rock star." CNNMoney website, May 1, 2004. Available online. URL: http://money. cnn.com/2004/05/01/pf/buffett_meeting/index.htm. Downloaded May 21, 2004.

———. "What Warren Buffett wants you to know." CNNMoney website, May 3, 2004. Available online. URL: http://money.cnn.com/2004/05/03/pf/buffett_qanda/ index.htm. Downloaded May 20, 2004.

ORGANIZATION

At the Berkshire Hathaway website you will find links to _A Message from Warren E. Buffett, Annual Reports - 1995 – 2003_ and _Warren Buffett's Letters to Berkshire Shareholders 1977 – 2003_, as well as several other related links.

Berkshire Hathaway

1440 Kiewit Plaza

Omaha, NE 68131

http://www.berkshirehathaway.com

FINANCE GLOSSARY

annual report business publication that reviews a company's activities over the preceding year

assets items listed on a company's balance sheet that show the value of its properties

balance sheet statement showing a company's financial condition on a given date

bear market condition in the stock market when stocks are declining in value

bond certificate of indebtedness, usually bearing interest

book value value of a business as shown by its balance sheet

bracket (or tax bracket) one of a graded series of income groups (for example, the $40,000 income bracket versus the $50,000 bracket)

bull market condition in the stock market when stock prices are rising

capital goods or money gathered by a business or an individual (that is, a capitalist)

cash flow money coming into a business

commission fee paid to a person who arranges and handles details of a sale

conglomerate corporation that owns smaller corporations

earnings balance of income that remains after costs and expenses have been deducted

foundation permanent organization that sets money aside for future use, usually for charitable purposes

inflation period in which the general level of prices rises significantly

interest charge for borrowing money that is usually a percentage of the amount borrowed

investment money that is spent to produce income or profit

liabilities debts

liquidate to change assets into cash

merger the combining of two or more organizations, such as businesses, into one

monopoly single or exclusive ownership

mutual fund investment company that invests its shareholders' money in a variety of other corporations

net worth the financial worth of an individual after liabilities have been deducted from assets

Op-Ed usually used to identify an essay written to appear on the page opposite the editorial page in a newspaper

portfolio any group of stocks or bonds held by an investor

recession period when economic activity is reduced

share(s) one or more of the equal parts into which the capital stock of a corporation is divided

shareholder person who owns one or more shares in a corporation.

stockbroker person who acts as an agent for a company that wishes to sell shares of its ownership or for an individual who wishes to buy shares

subsidiary company that is entirely controlled by another company

takeover act of taking over control or possession of a company

Wall Street street in New York City that is at the center of the "financial district"; more broadly, a term that refers to the banking and financial industry

INDEX

Page numbers in *italics* indicate illustrations.

ABOUT THE AUTHOR

Bernard Ryan, Jr., has authored, co-authored, or ghost-written 33 books on such topics as biography, early childhood education, community service for teens, career guides in the fields of advertising and journalism, courtroom trials, and personal financial planning, including four other books in the Ferguson Career Biographies series: *Condoleezza Rice: Secretary of State*; *Hillary Rodham Clinton: First Lady and Senator*; *Stephen Hawking: Physicist and Educator*; and *Jeff Bezos: Business Executive and Founder of Amazon.com*. His *Tyler's Titanic* is an early chapter book about what happens when a boy finds a way to visit the wreckage of the great ship on the ocean floor. In *The Wright Brothers: Inventors of the Airplane*, he tells the sixth- to ninth-grade reader the Wrights' life stories and explains how they brought the world the miracle of flight. His *Helping Your Child Start School* is an introduction to kindergarten for parents. *Simple Ways to Help Your Kids Become Dollar-Smart*, co-authored with financial planner Elizabeth Lewin, helps parents teach children, ages seven to 18, how to handle money. His *The Poisoned Life of Mrs. Maybrick* is the biography of an American woman who, in Liverpool, England, in 1889, was the defendant in one of history's great murder trials. Mr. Ryan has written many shorter pieces for magazine and newspaper publication, and is a graduate of The Rectory School, Kent School, and Princeton University. A native of Albion, New York, he lives with his wife, Jean Bramwell Ryan, in Southbury, Connecticut. They have two daughters and two grandchildren.